FROM CALEDONIA
TO THE PAMPAS

mpas

FROM CALEDONIA TO THE PAMPAS

Two Accounts by
Early Scottish Emigrants to the Argentine

•

William Grierson, 'The Voyage of the *Symmetry*'
'Faith Hard Tried': The Memoir of Jane Robson

•

Edited by Iain A. D. Stewart

TUCKWELL PRESS

First published in Great Britain in 2000 by
Tuckwell Press
The Mill House
Phantassie
East Linton
East Lothian EH40 3DG
Scotland

ISBN 1 86232 076 4

The publishers wish to thank the Scotland Inheritance Fund
for support in the publication of this volume

British Library Cataloguing in Publication Data

A catalogue record for this book is available
on request from the British Library

Typeset by Hewer Text Ltd, Edinburgh
Printed and bound by Cromwell Press, Trowbridge, Wiltshire

For my mother, Muriel Harvey Stewart,
and to the memory of Douglas Juan Gifford

CONTENTS

LIST OF ILLUSTRATIONS

ACKNOWLEDGEMENTS

Firstly, and most importantly, I extend my sincerest thanks to May and Hilda Dodds of Turdera, Province of Buenos Aires, for providing copies of 'The Voyage of the *Symmetry*' and 'Faith Hard Tried', and for allowing me the use of the latter, a family document, in my research. I am very grateful to those who have provided inspiration, counsel, and support throughout my investigations into the nineteenth-century Río de la Plata, especially Bernard Bentley, Nigel Dennis, Will Fowler, Louise Haywood, Alan Paterson, and Gustavo San Román, all of the Department of Spanish of the University of St Andrews, and Jason Wilson, Professor of Latin American Studies at University College London. Thanks are also due to Roger Mason of the Department of Scottish History at St Andrews for first suggesting that I should approach the publisher of the present volume, and to John Tuckwell for his advice and co-operation during its preparation. Last, but by no means least, I acknowledge the generous financial assistance received at various stages of my research from the Carnegie Trust for the Universities of Scotland, the Douglas Gifford Travel Scholarship, the School of Modern Languages of the University of St Andrews, and the Stewart Society.

INTRODUCTION

A Scottish traveller may today visit any corner of the globe and reasonably expect to find a number of compatriots residing there. Indeed, it seems that there are more full-blooded Scots and those claiming Scottish descent scattered around the world than there are remaining in their distant, but fondly remembered, homeland. As one observer notes, 'the Wandering Scot has become as much a part of history as the Wandering Jew or the Wandering Scholar'.[1] The Caledonian diaspora began in earnest, of course, with the Highland clearances during the decades following the Hanoverian triumph over the Jacobites at Culloden in 1746, when many of the displaced crofters were obliged to seek a new life overseas. In later years, further waves of Scots moved abroad driven by ambition rather than by dispossession or abject poverty. Some of these emigrants rose to high positions in colonial society, becoming the administrators and financiers who played so central a role in the expansion of the Empire; others sought their fortunes outside Great Britain's domain in the developing United States.

But numerous Scots headed elsewhere. In spite of the awareness of their overseas brethren that has long existed among Scots who stayed at home, those who ventured to Latin America are seldom remembered. Three identifiable factors have contributed to this neglect: 1) South America is still a largely forgotten and much misunderstood continent from the Northern European perspective; 2) although their economic and cultural influence became considerable, the number of Scots venturing there was always small compared to other areas; 3) the majority of those who made the voyage did so as sojourners rather than immigrants, that is, they travelled there to undertake a job of work and moved on after its completion. Typical of this category were the engineers who surveyed, constructed, and operated the region's first railways, or the men from the Highlands and Islands who found employment on the sheep stations of

1. John Walker (ed.), *The Scottish Sketches of R. B. Cunninghame Graham* (Edinburgh: Scottish Academic Press, 1982), p. 135.

Patagonia in the early part of the twentieth century.[2] However, some
Scots did settle permanently and the present volume brings together for
the first time two records of the experiences of such emigrants, one
relating the voyage made by a party from Leith to Buenos Aires in 1825
(William Grierson, 'The Voyage of the *Symmetry*'), and the other taking
the form of a personal account of the lifetime spent in Argentina by a
member of this group ('Faith Hard Tried': The Memoir of Jane Robson).

To settle in the River Plate region during the 1820s was certainly a
bold move. Throughout much of the nineteenth century, the evolving
Argentinian nation was plagued by outbreaks of civil conflict, the
consequence of social and political divisions which had emerged during
the process of emancipation from Spain. At the root of nearly all such
upheaval lay the disparity between the bourgeois ethos of the urban elite
and the traditional lifestyle of the rural population and lower classes. The
intelligentsia of Buenos Aires were ardent followers of the latest cultural
and ideological imports from Europe, whereas expert horsemanship and
the ability to dispatch an adversary, human or animal, with a swift flourish
of the knife were attributes of greater prestige to the common creole.[3] In
the years following Argentina's first steps towards independence in 1810,
the educated men of the city dominated the political sphere, but were
engaged in a constant struggle to defend their pre-eminence from attack
by regional strongmen, the caudillos. These charismatic, populist leaders
embodied the values of the ordinary citizen and despised the patronising
demeanour of the urban oligarchy, whose ideology, a blend of ration-
alism, economic liberalism, and social elitism, was an uneasy bedfellow of
the conservative, Hispanic beliefs of the majority.

The conflict was not only one of culture and style: the opposing sectors

2. For a description of the activities of a Scottish railroad builder in Latin
   America, see Craig Mair, *David Angus: The Life and Adventures of a Victorian
   Railway Engineer* (Stevenage: The Strong Oak Press, 1989). A brief account of
   the many shepherds who left the Isle of Lewis to work for an interval or to
   settle in southern Argentina and Chile has been published recently; see Greta
   Mackenzie, *Why Patagonia?* (Stornoway: *Stornoway Gazette*, 1995).
3. A succinct definition of the term 'creole' relevant to the River Plate region is
   offered by Benedict Anderson in *Imagined Communities: Reflections on the Origin
   and Spread of Nationalism*, revised edn (London: Verso, 1991): 'Creole (*Criollo*)
   – person of (at least theoretically) pure European descent but born in the
   Americas (and, by later extension, anywhere outside Europe)' (p. 47).

also had very different plans for the shape of the nascent republic. The liberal thinkers of the city became known as Unitarians on account of their project to build a single national entity with its capital in Buenos Aires. They were opposed by the more conservative Federalists, who favoured a loose alliance of semi-autonomous provinces. The Unitarians were ascendant during much of the 1820s, until war with Brazil over the sovereignty of the Banda Oriental (modern Uruguay) precipitated the collapse of Bernardino Rivadavia's government in 1827.

After the fall of the Unitarian administration, Manuel Dorrego, a Federalist, was elected to the governorship of Buenos Aires, the chief political office in Argentina until the creation of the national presidency in 1862. One of Dorrego's first actions after taking power was to invite British diplomatic mediation in an effort to resolve the dispute with Brazil. As a result of the intervention of Lord Ponsonby, Buenos Aires and Rio de Janeiro rescinded their claims to the territory on the eastern shore of the Plate, facilitating the creation of the independent República Oriental del Uruguay in 1828. Dorrego was soon to become the victim of his own initiative. Freed from their positions in the Banda Oriental under the terms of Ponsonby's treaty, two Unitarian generals, Juan Lavalle and José María Paz, revolted against the Federalist authorities. The unfortunate governor was captured by Lavalle and executed in cold blood. Civil war ensued, before the Federalists emerged victorious in 1829. At the end of that year, Juan Manuel de Rosas, a wealthy *estanciero* (cattle-rancher) and army commander, was elevated to the governorship with the extraordinary powers required to restore stability. For the next two decades, Rosas dominated Argentine politics and ruled with a rod of iron. Opposition was in no way tolerated (the Unitarians were berated in official propaganda as 'vile', 'filthy', 'savage', or 'perverse') and many of the dictator's adversaries fled into exile; others who remained to conspire against him were put to death.

The issue of European influence was central to the Unitarian–Federalist debate. Whilst in power, the Unitarians had translated their admiration for foreign culture into a programme to mould the young republic according to the precedents established by modern European nations, particularly Britain and France. Their attempts to impose comparable systems of government and social organisation on Argentina were complicated, however, by the essential characteristics of the local population. Only a tiny minority of creoles possessed even the most rudimentary learning and virtually all were unaccustomed to the notion of democracy. Hence, liberal thinkers gradually developed a consciousness of the need to educate the people, though their idea of education frequently had more in common with indoctrination than an attempt to open minds.

As a means of preparing fertile ground for the propagation of seeds sown by imported ideologies, education was, by its very nature, a long-term strategy. But Argentina needed a rapid solution. How better to implant these much-admired concepts and institutions, the early liberals began to ask, than to introduce them wholesale within their most natural medium, the citizen of modern Europe? This solution seemed remarkably straightforward and the Unitarian governments of the 1820s devised schemes to attract immigrants to the shores of the Plate. The impatience of the authorities, however, was to prove the downfall of this vision. Insufficient planning, together with the rash disregard of pledges of assistance made to potential settlers, endangered otherwise promising ventures. It was under the allure of one such scheme that the Scottish emigrants we are concerned with embarked for Buenos Aires.

A brief history of the Monte Grande colony

As part of their effort to attract British settlement and investment, the Buenos Aires government engaged Hullett and Company as their London agents.[4] The first major settlement proposal received by Hullett's was that of J. T. Barber Beaumont, whose initial inquiries in 1822 regarding the establishment of a British agricultural colony brought generous offers of assistance from Bernardino Rivadavia, then Minister of Government and Foreign Affairs.[5] Whilst on a diplomatic mission to Europe in 1824, Rivadavia consolidated his links with Barber Beaumont and the final terms of the colonisation plan were agreed. Early the

---

4. On Hullett's dealings with Buenos Aires, see H. S. Ferns, *Britain and Argentina in the Nineteenth Century* (Oxford: Clarendon Press, 1960), especially pp. 116-17 and 138.

5. Details of Barber Beaumont's scheme are recorded in J. A. B. Beaumont's *Travels in Buenos Ayres and the Adjacent Provinces of the Río de la Plata with Observations intended for the use of Persons who Contemplate Emigrating to that Country or Embarking Capital in its Affairs* (London: James Ridgway, 1828), especially Chapter 5 (pp. 99-131). The author was Barber Beaumont's son.

following year, while the first group of emigrants was preparing for departure, the Minister's secretary, Ignacio Núñez, published a pamphlet elaborating the support which the settlers could expect from the government. Among many other beneficial provisions, this document contained guarantees that the immigrants would be lodged in a 'commodious house' on arrival in Argentina for a period of fifteen days, that they would 'remain free from all military and civil service', and that their right to freedom of worship would be respected (cited by Beaumont, pp. 102–04).

The publicity surrounding Barber Beaumont's scheme attracted further proposals, including that of John and William Parish Robertson, two enterprising Scottish brothers with a long-standing involvement in the River Plate region. The organisation of a Scottish agricultural colony on Argentine soil had originally been suggested by Daniel Mackinlay, a leading figure in the early British merchant community of Buenos Aires.[6] Mackinlay fell seriously ill before he could bring the plan to fruition, but his idea reached the attention of the Parish Robertsons, probably through a mutual business partner, Thomas Fair. The brothers, natives of Kelso in the Scottish Borders, adopted Mackinlay's brainchild as their own. Early in 1825, they entered into a contract with the Buenos Aires authorities similar to that signed by Barber Beaumont, whose recruits were now ready to sail. By May, however, when the Scottish entrepreneurs were putting the finishing touches to their arrangements, Barber Beaumont's venture had already reached the point of collapse. On arriving in Buenos Aires, the first wave of settlers discovered that no land had been set aside for their colony, contrary to the previous declarations of the government. After a long delay in the capital, during which time the authorities toyed with the idea of sending the hapless immigrants 'to an *island in the River Negro*, among the *Patagonian Indians*', the settlers were finally allowed to proceed to the site originally promised near the frontier of Buenos Aires Province (Beaumont, p. 120, his italics). But on reaching this destination, they were met by a government official who informed them that they could not take possession of the land as he had 'lost the grant out of his pocket' and that he could not permit them to continue without the requisite paperwork (Beaumont, p. 121). Abandoned with no shelter or

6. Andrew Graham-Yooll, *The Forgotten Colony: A History of the English-Speaking Communities in Argentina* (London: Hutchinson, 1981), p. 163.

provisions, the majority of the party returned to the city and joined the British community there.

The authorities had also offered land to the Parish Robertsons, but the brothers considered the tract assigned to them to be of insufficient quality. Instead, according to material reproduced in James Dodds's *Records of the Scottish Settlers in the River Plate and their Churches*, the Parish Robertsons invested around '60,000 hard dollars' of their own resources to purchase 'three contiguous Chacras, or farms'.[7] The land, comprising some 16,660 acres within the modern districts of Lomas de Zamora and Esteban Echeverría in the Province of Buenos Aires, was purchased from the Scottish brothers John and George Gibson, the proprietors of several *estancias* (ranches) in the region.[8] The colony was officially titled Santa Catalina, after one of the original *chacras*, but is remembered as Monte Grande (large wood or orchard), the popular name of its site. Santa Catalina, the dwelling that became the Parish Robertsons' home, is now the head office of the University of Lomas de Zamora.[9]

Dodds recalls that prospective settlers were recruited in the spring of 1825 from 'the quiet hamlets and granges on the banks and braes o' bonnie Doon, the dales of the sweet winding Nith, the Annan, the Teviot . . . Ettrick's bonnie birken shaws, and the dowie dens o' Yarrow,

7. James Dodds, *Records of the Scottish Settlers in the River Plate and their Churches* (Buenos Aires: Grant and Sylvester, 1897), p. 38. Dodds was a prominent member of the Argentine-Scottish community in the latter part of the nineteenth century. On the Monte Grande colony, see also Cecilia Grierson, *Colonia de Monte Grande: Primera y única colonia formada por escoceses en la Argentina* (Buenos Aires: Peuser, 1925). Large sections of this work consist of material sourced from Dodds's volume, but rendered in Spanish. Cecilia was a granddaughter of William Grierson, author of 'The Voyage of the *Symmetry*', and she became Argentina's first female doctor of medicine.

8. In *The History and Present State of the Sheep-Breeding Industry in the Argentine Republic* (Buenos Aires: Ravenscroft and Mills, 1893), Herbert Gibson records that his family sold the property to 'Messrs. Robertson, who founded there the famous Scotch colony, and later on resold the land to Mr. William Fair' (p. 243). On the early history of the Gibsons, see Iain A. D. Stewart, 'Living with Dictator Rosas: Argentina through Scottish Eyes', *Journal of Latin American Studies* 29 (1997), 23-44.

9. William Denis Grant, 'A History of St. Andrew's Presbyterian Church in Argentina, Chapter 1', in the November-December 1989 issue of the newsletter of the Iglesia Presbiteriana San Andrés, Buenos Aires, pp. 8-11 (pp. 8-9). Thanks to Malcolm Gibson of Olivos, Province of Buenos Aires, for making this material available.

all so celebrated in song and romance' (p. 6). The emigrants congregated in Edinburgh in May 1825 and set sail from Leith on board the *Symmetry*. Dodds states that the colonists 'numbered more or less, 250 souls including children' (p. 11), but this figure embraces some who made their way to Buenos Aires independently. No records remain of the latter, nor of the identity of the vessels on which they sailed. The *Symmetry* party was composed of eight farmers and their families, an architect, a doctor, a bailiff, and the many tradesmen and servants required to establish and staff the colony (see passenger list on pp. 20–23 of this Introduction).

On arriving in Argentina, the settlers possessed only the most basic knowledge of the society they were about to join, a fact recorded by one of their number. En route to Buenos Aires, an unidentified member of the party wrote a poetic account of his voyage under the *nom de plume* 'Tam o' Stirling'.[10] Though humorous in tone, his verses reflect issues of serious concern to the naïve emigrants. As they near South America, Tam notes the wild speculation rife amongst his fellow passengers:

> They wondered what people the Argentines were,
> Savage or civilised – colour, and figure,
> And lassies resolved they would droon themselves ere
> They'd gang without claes or be kissed by a nigger.

On landing at the port, they were confused by their surroundings and mystified by linguistic difference:

> The *Symmetry* anchored, boats gathered around them,
> While jabbering foreigners their luggage received,
> The Babel o' tongues was enough to confound them,
> But naebody understood Scotch, they perceived.

It is hard for the modern reader of the settlers' accounts to fully appreciate their emotions on reaching the River Plate. The world must have seemed so much larger and more mysterious in the 1820s than it does in the age of efficient global travel and communications. By leaving Scotland, the emigrants had effectively crossed their personal Rubicon; even a visit home was a daunting if not impossible prospect, the uncomfortable sea voyage being costly and of around ten weeks'

---

10. The poem is reproduced as an Appendix to the present volume, pp. 117–21.

Bueno Aires and Surrounding Area.
MG = approximate site of Monte Grande colony

duration. The virtual irreversibility of their decision is suggested in Tam's poem, where Argentina is described as 'their land of adoption, home of the stranger, / From where they would ne'er go to sea any more'.

After only a few days in the city of Buenos Aires, the Scots proceeded to the Monte Grande site, where, against all the odds, they quickly established a thriving settlement. Their initial success is recorded in an article in the local English-language newspaper, *The British Packet*, of 25 October 1828:

> the colony not only soon laid the foundation of a permanent prosperity, but in two years entirely changed the face of that part of the country which it occupied, and at this moment the colony presents to the view of every one the realisation of all that the proprietors could propose – a model of industry, comfort, agricultural improvement, and moral excellence worthy of imitation, and highly creditable to the parties who have produced this happy result. (cited by Dodds, p. 38)

A comparable image of the settlers' existence is presented by the Argentinian author and statesman Domingo Faustino Sarmiento in his classic work of literature *Facundo* (1845). Early in this politically charged essay-cum-biography-cum-novel, Sarmiento depicts the Scottish and German communities in Buenos Aires Province as shining examples of civilised living. The industrious immigrants inhabited clean, well-kept homes:

> las casitas son pintadas, el frente de la casa siempre aseado, adornado de flores y arbustillos graciosos; el amueblado sencillo, pero completo, la vajilla de cobre o estaño reluciente siempre, la cama con cortinillas graciosas; y los habitantes en un movimiento y acción continuo. Ordeñando vacas, fabricando mantequilla y quesos, han logrado algunas familias hacer fortunas colosales y retirarse a la ciudad a gozar de las comodidades.[11]

> (their little houses are painted, the facades are always neat, adorned with flowers and attractive bushes, their furnishings are simple but adequate, their pots of copper or tin are always gleaming, the beds have elegant drapes, and the inhabitants are in a state of perpetual movement and activity. By milking cows, making butter and cheeses, some families have managed to make sizeable fortunes and to retire to enjoy the comforts of city life.)

Additionally, in the final chapter of *Facundo*, Sarmiento refers to the peaceable disposition of the Monte Grande colonists in support of his argument that a nation enhanced by the influx of 'civilised' immigrants would no longer be riven by internal conflict. Having claimed that 'con un millón de hombres civilizados la guerra civil es imposible; porque serían menos los que se hallarían en estado de desearla' ('civil war is impossible with a million civilised men, for those who desire it would find themselves in the minority') (p. 372), he cites the conduct of the Scottish settlers as proof of this assertion: 'La Colonia escocesa que Rivadavia fundó al sur de Buenos Aires lo prueba hasta la evidencia; ha sufrido de la guerra, pero ella jamás ha tomado parte' ('The Scottish colony founded by Rivadavia to the south of Buenos Aires is the evidence which proves this point; it suffered as a result of war, but it never took part in it') (p. 372).

11. Domingo Faustino Sarmiento, *Facundo* (Madrid: Cátedra, 1993), p. 64.

By 1826, the colony was already flourishing to the extent that the appointment of a minister and teacher was deemed necessary. To this end, the recently ordained Reverend William Brown was engaged to establish a Presbyterian mission at Monte Grande and to provide education for the colonists' children. Brown had been born in the Fife village of Leuchars in 1800 and had attended the grammar school and university in nearby St Andrews, before completing his theological studies at Aberdeen. In 1850, after working tirelessly for the spiritual benefit of the Argentine-Scots community and playing an instrumental role in the foundation of the Scots School in Buenos Aires, an establishment which exists to this day, he returned to Scotland and was appointed to the Chair of Divinity and Biblical Criticism at the University of St Andrews, a position he occupied with distinction until his death in 1868.[12]

Despite their initial achievements, the settlers' circumstances soon took a turn for the worse. The unstable economic climate arising from the war with Brazil and the fall of the Unitarian government militated against their prosperity. The final straw was the struggle between Rosas's Federalists and the Unitarians commanded by Lavalle. In May 1829, the countryside around Monte Grande was occupied by forces of both factions and, fearing for their lives, most of the settlers fled to the city of Buenos Aires or to other parts of the Province. Harassment by marauding bands of troops was to remain a threat to those Scots who persisted in rural areas during the Rosas era. In one incident, described by Dodds, soldiers robbed a house and attempted to murder its occupant, James

---

12. A detailed account of the life of William Brown is provided by Dodds, pp. 201-10. Little record of Brown remains in the archives of the University of St Andrews, aside from the periodic appearance of his name in the minutes of Senate meetings and a few traces of his undergraduate career, such as the fact that he was joint recipient of the Gray Prize in 1817. In Brown's obituary in *The Scotsman* (reproduced by Dodds, pp. 202-03), some details of his influence in St Andrews and beyond are noted: 'Under his direction the Divinity Hall at St. Andrews was for many years a leading centre of intellectual activity, and he was one of the first who laid the foundation of the Liberal party in the Church, particularly in the direction of philosophical speculation'. In the same notice it is stated that 'he published almost nothing from a fastidious dread of print'. For an analysis of one of Brown's sermons, focusing upon its implications for the religious outlook of the early Scottish settlers, see Iain A. D. Stewart, 'Textual Representations of Religion in Rosas' Argentina', *Bulletin of Hispanic Studies* 74 (1997), 483-500 (pp. 494-97).

Miller (pp. 54-55). On another occasion, the Robsons' property was assaulted and, when confronted by young John Robson, 'one of the wretches raised his blunderbuss and shot him in the face, and then each with his sword (four of them) stabbed him to death' (Dodds, p. 56).[13]

Rosas and the British settlers

So Rosas came to power. Soon his hold
Gripped the whole land as though it were a horse.
Church, Money, Law, all yielded. He controlled
That land's wild passions with his wilder force.
And through their tears men heard from time to time
His slaves at worship of his clever crime.[14]

Victory over the Unitarian rebels during the civil war merely enhanced Juan Manuel de Rosas's already burgeoning status as the most powerful figure in Buenos Aires and made his election to the governorship in December 1829 a formality. Although he had previously resisted deep involvement in institutional politics, his family background and early life had prepared him well for elevation to executive office. On the side of his father, Rosas was descended from high colonial officials, including a former governor of Buenos Aires. His maternal grandfather, a wealthy rancher, had been a leading figure in the militia and had died defending his property from an Indian attack. When only eighteen, Rosas became manager of his father's *estancia*, thereby acquiring the traditional skills which later guaranteed popularity amongst the gauchos and helped to secure their overwhelming support for his regime.[15] In 1813, against the

13. Here Dodds relied upon the testimony of Mrs Jane Robson (née Rodger), more than a decade before she referred to this murder in 'Faith Hard Tried' (pp. 80-81). Jane was a child at the time of the attack. The unfortunate John Robson had a brother named Hugh who later became Jane's husband.

14. John Masefield, 'Rosas', in *The Collected Poems of John Masefield* (London: William Heinemann, 1932), pp. 503-21 (p. 510).

15. Sarmiento reminds us of Rosas's gauchesque capabilities in *Facundo*: 'El general Rosas, dicen, conoce por el gusto el pasto de cada estancia del sur de Buenos Aires' ('General Rosas, they say, knows by taste the grass of every ranch of the southern part of Buenos Aires Province') (p. 86). This skill is associated with the *baqueano*, a gaucho expert in finding directions.

wishes of his parents, he married Encarnación Ezcurra, who, until her premature death in 1838, played a leading role in her husband's public career. Shortly after the marriage, Rosas abandoned his post at the family ranch and set out to seek his fortune. Along with two friends, he founded one of the earliest *saladeros* (beef-salting plants) in Argentina. The business flourished and Rosas invested the profits in his first *estancia*, Los Cerrillos.[16] With a sound financial base, a private gaucho battalion, and the enthusiastic backing of fellow landowners and members of the impoverished underclass, both of whom coveted the bulwark he represented against the meddling of the urban bourgeoisie, Rosas was ideally placed to eclipse all rivals for years to come.

On 5 December 1832, however, Rosas completed his first term of office as governor and resisted pressure to stand for re-election. Instead, he supported the candidacy of Juan Ramón Balcarce, who was duly elected by the House of Representatives. Once in power, Balcarce attempted to distance himself from the Rosista faction and undermined its supremacy. During 1833, whilst Rosas was leading the so-called Desert Campaign against the Indian tribes, the new governor openly turned against the Rosistas and drove a few hundred of their number out of Buenos Aires, only for them to retaliate by laying siege to the city. Doña Encarnación organised internal resistance to her husband's opponents until Balcarce was obliged to concede defeat and resign. Two short-lived administrations followed, but Rosas was persuaded to return to the governorship in 1835. Previous refusals to resume office stood Rosas in good stead, as the popular clamour for his return had become so great that he could now demand to be installed on his own terms, namely that he be granted *la suma del poder público* (maximum public power). Rosas insisted that the appointment should be approved by referendum and, though he enjoyed genuine popularity, the staggering result of the vote probably owed much to electoral intimidation, as there was no secrecy of ballot. Only four votes were recorded against Rosas in the plebiscite, with 9,316 in his favour.[17]

---

16. On Rosas's early years, see Carlos Ibarguren, *Juan Manuel de Rosas: su vida, su tiempo, su drama*, 2nd edn (Buenos Aires: Roldán, 1930), pp. 5-65. Other important biographies/histories include Manuel Gálvez, *Vida de don Juan Manuel de Rosas* (Buenos Aires: Fontis, 1975) and John Lynch, *Argentine Dictator: Juan Manuel de Rosas 1829-1852* (Oxford: Clarendon Press, 1981).
17. These figures are given by Lynch, *Argentine Dictator*, p. 163.

The ethos of Rosas's governorships differed radically from that of the Unitarian administrations of the mid-1820s. Ideological imports no longer held sway; on the contrary, Rosas cultivated an aura of nationalism which scorned docile adherence to foreign models. In place of the Unitarians' devotion to modern European ideas and culture, Rosas sought a return to traditional values. In the rhetoric of the regime, these were increasingly portrayed as authentically 'American', and thus representative of the noble ideals of independence and self-determination, although most bore close resemblance to the traditions of colonial Spain. The Catholic Church, for example, regained (in appearances, at least) much of the power and prestige which Rivadavia had attempted to strip away from it, and religious doctrine again played a central part in everyday life.

Another upshot of the change in political atmosphere was that European settlers were no longer considered a panacea for Argentina's ills on account of their cultural background, and the active promotion of immigration ceased. On the other hand, Rosas recognised that he could not afford to isolate the outsider nor mistreat the existing settlers, for the Argentine economy relied upon good relations with foreign powers and was particularly dependent on a lucrative trading alliance with Britain.[18] Naturally, this situation meant that the British government also had a vested interest in maintaining an *entente cordiale*, to the extent that when the French navy blockaded Buenos Aires between 1838 and 1840 during a dispute with the dictator, the Foreign Office sought to end the intervention through diplomatic channels.

Between 1836 and 1845, Britain's policy towards Rosas was influenced by the personal bias of John Henry Mandeville, the British representative in Buenos Aires, who favoured the dictator to the degree that John Lynch has suggested that he 'was more than sympathetic; he was almost partisan'.[19] During the early years of Mandeville's mission, relations between London and Buenos Aires were generally good, supported by the liberal foreign policy of Viscount Melbourne's Whig administration. Throughout Palmerston's tenure of the post of Foreign Secretary, the approach towards Latin America was based upon reaching amicable

18. The foundations of Anglo-Argentine trade were set out in the Treaty of Amity, Commerce and Navigation signed by the two governments in 1825. The full text of this document is reproduced as an appendix to J. A. B. Beaumont's *Travels in Buenos Ayres* (pp. 263-70).
19. Lynch, *Argentine Dictator*, p. 264.

trading agreements to ensure favourable conditions for British commerce in the region.

In 1841, Robert Peel's Conservative government came to power and Palmerston was replaced by Lord Aberdeen. Peel assumed a tougher line towards the Rosas regime, triply motivated by the desire to mend relations with the French, by anger towards the dictator's apparent disregard of the Argentine national debt, most of which was held by British creditors, and by the attempts of Buenos Aires to restrict foreign navigation rights in the Paraná river. The death of the xenophobic dictator of Paraguay, Dr José Gaspar Rodríguez de Francia, in 1840 had rendered that nation ripe for commercial exploitation, an impossible development unless the Paraná was opened to shipping. Moreover, Rosas's increasing embroilment in an originally civil conflict in Uruguay was beginning to jeopardise mercantile activity in the River Plate. In an attempt to impose regional stability, Aberdeen instructed Mandeville to press the dictator into accepting British mediation, but the envoy's pro-Rosas sympathies soon became incompatible with the instructions of his government and he was recalled to Britain.

The new ambassador to Buenos Aires, William Gore Ouseley, was the antithesis of his predecessor and adopted an openly hostile approach to the Rosas regime, even calling for British military intervention. Having convinced Aberdeen of the need for assertive action, Ouseley, in conjunction with the French representative, Baron Deffaudis, engineered the Anglo-French blockade of Buenos Aires from 1845 to 1848. This measure was principally intended to put an end to Rosas's interference in the ongoing conflict in Uruguay, with the objectives of guaranteeing that nation's autonomy and ensuring it retained its status as a safe haven for European traders in the region. Rather than enhancing the prospects for commercial speculation, however, the blockade only served to damage Anglo-Argentine relations.[20]

20. On relations between the two countries during the 1830s and 1840s, see Lynch, *Argentine Dictator*, especially pp. 247-94, and Ferns, *Britain and Argentina in the Nineteenth Century*, pp. 240-80. For an account of the diplomatic manoeuvring associated with the Anglo-French blockade written from a pro-Rosas perspective, see José Luis Muñoz Azpiri, *Rosas frente al imperio británico* (Buenos Aires: Theoría, 1974). For a critique of the blockade from the point of view of one who wished for Rosas's demise, see José Luis Bustamante, *Los cinco errores capitales de la intervención anglo-francesa en el Plata* [Montevideo, 1849] (Buenos Aires: Solar, 1942).

In 1846, Peel's government fell and Palmerston returned to the Foreign Office under Lord John Russell's premiership. He considered that the blockade of Buenos Aires was unjust and that a French and British policy of obliging ships to dock in the port of Montevideo and pay duties there was 'piracy . . . equivalent to stopping neutral vessels on the high seas and making them pay blackmail'.[21] The new government rebuked Ouseley for his partisan stance and replaced him with Lord Howden. On 7 July 1847, Howden and his French counterpart, Walewski, reached an armistice agreement with Manuel Oribe, one of the protagonists of the Uruguayan conflict and a close ally of Rosas. Although the peace did not hold, the British resolved to withdraw from the Plate; the French, meanwhile, continued the blockade alone for a further year.

Despite the friction between London and Buenos Aires throughout the 1840s, most Britons residing in Argentina seem to have had little quarrel with the dictator. In the words of H. S. Ferns,

> The British merchants with an established interest in Argentina,
> and the Scottish and Irish sheep masters who came out during the
> 1830s and 1840s, found Rosas an agreeable enough politician. He
> kept order, he protected property and he made trade possible.[22]

Though broadly supportive of the regime, many settlers regarded Rosas with some suspicion and were alert to his volatile nature. Their cautious attitude becomes manifest in a memorandum sent by Ouseley to Lord Aberdeen, which is reproduced and discussed in a short article by Wilbur Devereux Jones.[23] According to Jones, Ouseley, shortly after arriving in Argentina in 1845, 'requested a number of British residents in Buenos Aires to describe the situation of the British colony for him, and the most informative of these replies he sent to Aberdeen' (p. 90). The envoy's intention was to assess the opinion of the Argentine-British community before advising any intervention against Rosas. Ouseley commends the contents of the document in the following terms:

21. Cited by Rory Miller, *Britain and Latin America in the Nineteenth and Twentieth Centuries* (London and New York: Longman, 1993), p. 52.
22. H. S. Ferns, 'Britain's Informal Empire in Argentina, 1806-1914', *Past and Present*, 4 (1954), 60-75 (p. 69).
23. Wilbur Devereux Jones, 'The Argentine British Colony in the Time of Rosas', *Hispanic American Historical Review*, 40 (1960), 90-97.

> This memm. is worth reading as containing the opinion of a
> conscientious unprejudiced man – deeply interested in the
> results of our proceedings in the River Plate, and in the fate of
> our countrymen. He is a Scotchman – he requested me not to
> name him as the author of this memorandum. (p. 90)

The author of the note divides the British population into three distinct
categories: merchants, farmers, and an artisan/labourer class. We are told
that the farmers are chiefly of Scottish or Irish origin and live in
settlements which 'have been formed during the last fifteen or twenty
years and comprise numerous families and individuals' (p. 91). On the
whole, it appears that the British population had been fortunate enough
to avoid severe hardships during the early years of the Rosas administration, but 'the tendency of the policy pursued towards them latterly, has
decidedly been intolerant, hostile and injurious' (p. 92). The main
concern of the settlers was that any instance of British intervention in
the region might place their lives and property at risk. In such an event, it
was those who dwelt in rural areas who were considered the most likely
to encounter danger:

> in view of the impending rupture between England and Buenos
> Ayres, the situation of the British whose property and residence
> are in the country, becomes peculiarly critical and delicate. If
> they abide in their homes, they must be the prey of habitual
> dread, and may be the victims of sudden and secret violence; if
> they abandon them, they reduce themselves to poverty and
> destitution; they cannot even remove to town without the risk
> of serious loss. They have no means of living apart from their
> herds and flocks; they cannot even live long in the city
> unprovided for, and least of all is it in their power to remove
> from the country and go elsewhere. They remain, not because
> they can remain with confidence and security, but because it is
> not in their power to remove. It is an aggravation of the evil in
> this case that they are the best and most respectable of the
> British, in a moral point of view (of those viz., settled in the
> country) that would suffer most; for they are the honest, the
> sober and the industrious who have gradually acquired property.
> (p. 92)

The solidarity and cohesion of the settler community is demonstrated in the memorandum; we are told, for example, that 'they come together at stated times from a circuit twenty or thirty miles in diameter for the purpose of divine worship' (p. 93). Despite the hazards posed by the prospect of war between Britain and Rosas, the author of the document does not seek to dissuade the British government from adopting this policy, asserting that the settlers will remain loyal British subjects whatever course of action is chosen. Nevertheless, his description of an industrious and morally upstanding settler community is followed by a clear warning that conflict between Britain and Argentina could destroy this lifestyle, a more than adequate implication that he favours a peaceful resolution to the crisis. The reader of the report is left in little doubt of the probable consequences of military conflict for the rural settlers:

> War between Buenos Ayres and England, and especially
> protracted war, would in all likelihood, as far as regards this
> portion of the British, be their virtual annihilation as Britons.
> They must either be ruined by abandoning the country
> altogether, or, by remaining, cease from their distinctive
> peculiarities, and gradually assimilate themselves in manners and
> ideas to the inhabitants of the country. (p. 93)

According to Jones's analysis, 'the end product of the document was to leave two alternatives open to the British government – an all-out war against Rosas, or a peace policy' (p. 96). 'A lingering intervention', Jones reasons, 'such as might ensue from a blockade, was held to be fraught with great dangers to the colonists' (p. 96). In addition, he claims that given Aberdeen's 'peace-loving' nature, it was inconceivable that he would have chosen war out of the two options suggested in the memorandum, concluding that, in effect, the document advocated a policy of reconciliation (p. 96). In a final piece of speculation, Jones casts further doubt over the authorship of the report, conjecturing that it may have been drafted as a clever piece of propaganda 'with the connivance of the dictator', although there is no strong historical evidence to support this verdict (pp. 96-97). Indeed, it seems improbable that Ouseley would have accepted the document had he detected even the vaguest hint of official meddling, especially in light of his personal bias against the regime and the fact that he was the main proponent of British intervention against Rosas.

To summarise, the settlers were understandably wary of Rosas's mode of government, but were more concerned that any disruption could pose a serious threat to their way of life. The occasional brush with the rougher elements amongst Rosas's supporters must have seemed a small price to pay for what was, by the standards of the time and place, a relatively stable political climate. Of all the foreign residents, support for the dictator was probably strongest among the English-speaking settlers, who shared his belief in civil discipline and were largely unimpressed by idealistic notions of liberty and social equality. Further evidence of this attitude can be seen in W. H. Hudson's *Far Away and Long Ago* (1918), an autobiographical work in which the elderly author and naturalist, who spent the majority of his adult life in England, recalls his distant youth as the son of North American settlers in Buenos Aires Province.

While much of *Far Away and Long Ago* relates the development of Hudson's passion for the study of nature, and ornithology in particular, he records in the seventh chapter his first visit to Buenos Aires as a young boy, the highlight of which was catching a glimpse of Rosas's jester, don Eusebio. This reminiscence leads Hudson to a consideration of the dictator himself, describing Rosas as 'the Nero of South America' and 'one of the bloodiest as well as the most original-minded of the Caudillos and Dictators, and altogether, perhaps, the greatest of those who have climbed into power in this continent of republics and revolutions'.[24] He reflects upon the fall of Rosas in the following chapter and here we can observe the typical pro-Rosas attitude of the settler embodied in the figure of Hudson's father, 'an out-and-out Rosista' (p. 108). Portraits of the dictator and his late wife took pride of place on the drawing-room wall of Hudson's boyhood home, 'flanked by the repellent, truculent countenance of the Captain-General Urquiza' and further likenesses of Manuel Oribe and the Minister of War (p. 109). In describing common opinions of Rosas, Hudson neatly encapsulates the views of the English-speaking settlers:

> People were in perpetual conflict about the character of the
> great man. He was abhorred by many, perhaps by most; others
> were on his side even for years after he had vanished from their
> ken, and among these were most of the English residents of the

---

24. W. H. Hudson, *Far Away and Long Ago: A Childhood in Argentina* (London: Century Hutchinson, 1985), pp. 105-06.

country, my father among them. Quite naturally I followed my father and came to believe that all the bloodshed during a quarter of a century, all the crimes and cruelties practised by Rosas, were not like the crimes committed by a private person, but were all for the good of the country, with the result that in Buenos Ayres and throughout our province there had been a long period of peace and prosperity, and that all this ended with his fall and was succeeded by years of fresh revolutionary outbreaks and bloodshed and anarchy. (pp. 126-27)

As Hudson indicates, the settlers' greatest fear was the chaos which they believed would be the inevitable result of the dictator's demise. Their worries seem to have been justified by Hudson's account of the aftermath of Caseros, the battle which ended Rosas's reign in 1852. A constant stream of defeated troops passed by the family's home, demanding food and horses in a threatening manner since there was no longer a superior authority to restrict their excesses. Hudson asserts that 'these men were now lawless and would not hesitate to plunder and kill in their retreat', and demonstrates that only the courage of his father when confronted by their menaces enabled the family to survive unscathed (p. 117). In the eyes of the foreign settlers, therefore, Rosas's draconian rule was the single check upon the inherent savageness of the common creole. Hudson, whilst clearly not condoning the worst brutality of the regime, considered Rosas's more heinous deeds the product of either 'sudden fits of passion or petulance', 'a peculiar, sardonic, and somewhat primitive sense of humour', or the socio-cultural milieu, the latter resonating the type of environmental determinism prevalent in the ideology of the dictator's liberal opponents (pp. 130-31).

The *Voyage of the* Symmetry

William Grierson's decision to keep a journal of the Monte Grande colonists' voyage to Buenos Aires, partly for his own satisfaction and partly for the benefit of his friends at home, has afforded us a fascinating account of the tribulations one could expect to experience on a long sea passage during the 1820s and an illuminating insight into the mixed emotions of those who leave their homeland in search of opportunity abroad. Grierson, one of the eight farmers who formed the nucleus of the party, embarked on this intrepid journey with his wife Catharine (or Catherine), their three children, and assorted farmyard animals (he mentions in the account that one of his sows gave birth to a litter of sixteen piglets during the voyage). Before commenting briefly on some features of Grierson's journal itself, it may be appropriate at this point to transcribe the passenger list of the *Symmetry* which James Dodds reconstructed from consular records (*Records of the Scottish Settlers*, pp. 18-20). Dodds qualifies the list in the following manner: 'These are the names of the colonists who received Consular protections after their arrival here, per ship *Symmetry*, but we know that some few of them also came out in other vessels, whose names we have not been able to trace' (p. 20). He does not claim, therefore, that his register is a comprehensive and entirely accurate inventory of either those who sailed on the *Symmetry* or of the residents of the Monte Grande colony, but it is, nonetheless, the most complete record we have today of the party which made the voyage and settled there. I also suspect that some duplication occurs in Dodds's list (e.g. Ebenezer Jaggart and Ebenezer Haggart; the two 26-year-old servants named Robert M'Clymont). The names of William and Catharine Grierson, James and Euphemia Rodger(s) (the parents of Jane Robson, née Rodger), and Hugh and Jane Robson (the parents of Jane Rodger's future husband) are highlighted in bold type.

MONTE GRANDE COLONY
PER SHIP 'SYMMETRY'

Sailed from Leith on the 22nd May, and arrived at Buenos Aires on the 11th August 1825.

Name	Age	Profession	Married	Children
David Anderson	50	farmer	Mary	2
James Broach	24	farmer	and sister[s][25]	
William Grierson	**32**	**farmer**	**Catherine**[26]	**3**

25. In 'The Voyage of the *Symmetry*', William Grierson makes reference to 'my female cousins, the two Miss Broaches' (20 May 1825), but Dodds's list indicates that there was only one.
26. Throughout Grierson's journal, the name of his wife is consistently spelt as 'Catharine', rather than the more usual 'Catherine'.

Name	Age	Profession	Married	Children
Thomas Galbraith	28	farmer	Jane	1
John M'Clymont	25	farmer	Catherine	2
John Miller	38	farmer	Anne	1
James White	24	farmer	Margaret	0
William White	22	farmer	Janet	1
James Aird	28	carpenter	Mary	1
Richard Adams	32	architect	Anna	4
John Goldsworthy	25	painter	Sylvia, governess	1
William Arthur	26	cooper	Margaret	1
William Steel	24	servant		
Anne Aird	19	servant		
William Attwell	43	basket-maker	Agnes	5
Robert Burns	28	trainer	Anne	1
Helen Bone	25	servant		
Robert Barclay	23	servant	Helen	1
James Brown	25	servant	Mary	1
Maxwell Beattie	21	servant		
William Burns	31	servant	Elizabeth	2
Margaret Barber	25	servant		
Robert Boyd	21	servant	Maria	0
Anne Irving	18	servant		
Ebenezer Jaggart	23	servant		
Ruth Irving	21	servant		
William Johnstone	36	servant		
Andrew Lawrie	24	carpenter	Helen	0
Edward Leach	19	bricklayer		
James Lawrie	22	blacksmith		
John Jarrell	21	servant		
Jane Jarrell	20	servant		
Peter Morton	27	servant	Mary	0
Alexander Malcolm	25	servant		
Susan M'Michan	23	servant		
D. M'Reavie	27	servant	Agnes	1
Thomas Mallet	29	bricklayer		
John Mitchell	25	butcher		
Thomas M'Kenzie	20	clerk		

Name	Age	Profession	Married	Children
John Moddick	30	servant		
Robert M'Gregor	22	seaman		
Robert M'Clymont	26	servant	Maria Boyd	0
Andrew Rae	30	servant	Anne	2
Hugh Robson	**43**	**servant**	**Jane**	**6**
James Rodger(s)	**28**	**servant**	**Euphemia**	**2**
Barbara Rankin	21	servant		
Malcolm Ramsay	16	clerk		
John Robertson	17	servant		
James Smith	23	bricklayer		
John Simpson	29	clerk	. . .	1
John Robson	18	servant		
Janet Brown	26	servant		
Moses Berry	22	carpenter		
Jonathan Barker	40	bricklayer	Elizabeth	2
Anne Crosby	18	governess		
William Crozier	32	servant	Anne	2
George Croughton	26	servant		
John Clark	28	servant		
Turnbull Clark	30	servant		
James Cathcart	23	surveyor		
Robert M'Clymont	26	servant		
William Chessell	25	carpenter		
William Martin Ennar	24	carpenter		
David Fleming	24	bootmaker	Margaret	1
Mungo Tinnock	22	servant		
Thomas Fulcher	22	sawyer		
William Goodman	25	bricklayer	Jane Smith	0
Thomas Griff	28	bricklayer	Laura	0
Thomas Grahame	25	servant	Martha	2
Joseph Grahame	27	servant	Ruth	0
John Gowan	27	servant	Sarah	0
Marion Hazell	25	servant		
Benjamin Hill	33	sawyer	Elizabeth	0
Thomas Heally	24	bricklayer		
John Hicks	26	bricklayer		

Name	Age	Profession	Married	Children
James Candlish Hart	27	carpenter	Hannah	1
William Young	23	servant	Barbara	1
Andrew Young	28	servant	Betsy	3
Elizabeth Hedger	25	servant		
Henry Innes	23	land surveyor		
John Taylor	30	carpenter		
John Tweedie	50	gardener	Janet Kings	6
Ebenezer Haggart	25	servant		
James Watson	30	servant	Catherine	0
Margaret Wright	26	servant		
John Watson	24	servant		
John Whitaker	41	painter	Maria Buist	2
James Purvis	21	servant		
Peter Purvis	19	servant		
William Speed	26	carpenter	Euphemia	1
John Christian	39	land surveyor		
Thomas Debenham	28	carpenter	Janet	6
Andrew Duncan	29	carpenter	Maggie	3
John Mair	19	blacksmith		
William Pixton	38	sawyer		
Thomas Bell	27	bailiff		
A. Kidd	34	servant	Jane	5
J. Smart	25	bricklayer		
George Dawson	30	servant	Jeanie	3
George Knight	29	sawyer	Eleonora	2
William Wilson	25	doctor		

Grierson's account of the voyage begins on 20 May 1825, as the *Symmetry* lies in Leith Roads, with a description of the commotion surrounding the final preparations for departure. The opening passages of Grierson's journal are imbued with not inconsiderable literary quality. Recalling the visit of 'our Employer's Father and Mother', the parents of John and William Parish Robertson, to the boat prior to setting sail, Grierson eloquently notes that 'the old gentleman was no novice in the Mysteries of Bacchus'. As the vessel slips from the Forth the following day, he pens an expressive farewell to his native land, avowing the emigrants' fidelity to the memory of Scotland and its traditions:

> Must we bid you adieu? We will bear you in our Breasts. We
> will look to the South. We will court your forms in distant
> climes. Our present children will prattle your names, and our
> future offspring shall learn your songs. When we have passed the
> Sun, when we have found what we may call a new heaven and
> a new earth, we will hold you in remembrance, and a third part
> of Earth's circumference shall not separate you from us, even
> when there (if ever we get there) our friendship shall operate;
> our mutual correspondence will demonstrate that our reciprocal
> *Love* is immortal. (22 May 1825)

Once at sea, Grierson's testimony becomes more prosaic, only regaining such poetic quality at the conclusion of the voyage, but it is no less interesting for this fact. He provides abundant information about daily life aboard, portrays the emigrants' activities and moods, makes meteorological observations, and records details of the *Symmetry*'s progress, often including readings of latitude and longitude. He describes the party's food, which appears to have been plentiful and of a more than adequate standard ('I never lived better, all my life. – we have fresh-pig, fine preserved soup . . . plenty of rice pudding, and fine flour for bread', 9 July 1825), their communal acts of worship on the Sabbath, a custom broken only when weather conditions were not conducive to gathering *en masse*, the argumentative disposition of the London bricklayers who accompanied the settlers, and the excitement with which the emigrants greeted passing vessels and exotic creatures of the deep.

Towards the end of the journal Grierson records his first impressions of Buenos Aires, which he summarises thus: 'I have observed that the Country seems bleak, the City gloomy, and the aspect of the Inhabitants rather forbidding' (11 August 1825). In the same entry, he asserts, however, that the settlers must leave behind their old prejudices in order to form 'proper, and consistent Ideas'. Though the closing paragraphs of his journal evoke nostalgia for the Scottish homeland, they contain no hint of regret. Rather, I believe we can detect an enthusiasm on Grierson's part to immerse himself in his new existence and to embrace the foreignness of Argentina in a spirit of adventure. Nonetheless, he still feels some trepidation about what lies ahead and harbours understandable reservations regarding the disposition of the local populace: 'I do not look upon the common appearance of the people, here, any way calculated to make the most favourable prepossessions; and any accounts that we hear of their manners, and conduct, do not belie their aspect' (8 August 1825). He wisely takes the widespread precaution of carrying firearms in the city.

While Grierson's account ends as the settlers disembark, 'Faith Hard Tried' opens by indicating some of the problems the Scots had to face soon after arrival. Although subtly different in genre from Grierson's record, in that it is a memoir composed in retrospect rather than an ongoing diary, this text provides equally significant insights into the settlers' existence. 'Faith Hard Tried' is the (auto)biography of Jane Robson (née Rodger), who arrived in Argentina on the *Symmetry* as a young girl with her sister and parents. Early in the twentieth century, towards the end of a long and eventful life and as one of the last remaining members of the party which had sailed from Leith over eighty years earlier, Jane recounted her past to an interested acquaintance, one M. R. Powell, who committed her experiences to paper for the benefit of future generations of the family. Whilst the process by which this text has survived its originator – through the filter of an amateur 'editor' – means that we must remain cautious of accepting it as Jane Robson's verbatim account, there is no reason to suspect that it offers anything other than an authentic rendition of her life story. In the following pages, a thematic approach to her text is adopted, with the aim of introducing the reader to a selection of its principal or recurrent concerns, issues which were probably of personal and collective relevance to most members of the early Argentine-Scottish community.

Themes in 'Faith Hard Tried': The Memoir of Jane Robson

1. General impressions of Argentina and the issue of subjectivity

We can only guess the view of Argentinian society formed by most of the early settlers, but the opinions set out in Jane Robson's account were probably quite typical. Base dishonesty, greed, and a lack of trustworthiness are the essential characteristics which Jane assigns to the average creole in the rural parts of Buenos Aires Province, an opinion only confirmed by a lifetime of bitter personal experiences at the hands of both officialdom and Argentinian neighbours. This view of the locals contrasts sharply with her rather idealistic conviction of the moral integrity of the Scottish community, an attitude deriving, perhaps, from a Presbyterian upbringing.

Jane opens her autobiography with a tale of deceit and double-dealing. Soon after arriving in Buenos Aires, her father decided to break away from the Monte Grande party for the simple reason that 'things were not as had been represented to him'. Although Jane does not elaborate upon the exact nature of her father's disillusionment, the explanation is likely to stem from the fact that the authorities failed to provide the generous financial assistance they had originally promised. Then, having set up on their own, the Rodger family immediately fell victim to the tricks of an unscrupulous local:

> Father started by buying a milk cow which promptly returned
> to its previous owner some distance across the camp. Father got
> it back, but the same thing happened again and on each
> occasion he had to buy it over again, or at any rate pay
> something, such was the dishonesty of those amongst whom we
> lived.

Brazen theft of this kind was supplemented by that of a more threatening nature. Jane recalls an attempt by 'three horrible rough looking men' to rob and kill her mother and a companion as they returned home from selling butter and cheese in the nearby town of Chascomús, a fate avoided only by leaving the road and riding through the tall dense thistles which flourished in that part of the Province. During the civil war of 1828 to 1829, the Rodgers' property was frequently visited by 'wandering ruffians', who, on one occasion, attacked an employee of the family, intimidated Jane's mother, and killed their dog by 'cutting him to the backbone in three places' with a sword. Worse would probably have followed but for the fortuitous arrival of a neighbour and the proximity of a contingent of rival troops.

It was not only the nature of the creole population which the new arrivals found disconcerting; the incomers were largely unprepared for such mundane factors as climatic difference and the reversal of the seasons in the southern hemisphere, discoveries which only intensified their feeling of vulnerability and provoked nostalgic recollections of home.

Jane Robson vividly states the awe inspired by unfamiliar meteorological phenomena throughout her account. She recalls as a young girl being struck on the neck by an 'aire', which is described as 'a shock of bad air . . . [that] often causes great damage; it will crack or shatter a mirror, glasses, etc.'. Whilst the scientific grounding of this observation is dubious (her neck was probably affected by nothing more than a draught, but a localised air current of such destructive potential is of questionable veracity), it serves to attribute a dimension of mysterious, unseen power to the Argentine environment, thus boosting the implicit pioneer myth that pervades Jane's story and casts the settlers' enterprise as an heroic crusade against a conspiracy of unfriendly locals and hostile natural forces. Similarly, Jane's descriptions of fearsome storms, although presented in a deadpan style, smack of hyperbole. At one point, she tells of a ferocious wind which blew livestock away, claiming that 'one man estimated that his sheep had been carried by the wind for about 30 leagues'. On another occasion, Jane recalls being hit by lightning during her childhood, an accident which left her unconscious 'for some hours'.

Such memories, which to some degree evoke the magical realism encountered in modern Spanish American fiction, stretch the bounds of credibility despite the very matter-of-fact manner in which they are related and suggest a rather carefree approach on the part of the speaker to danger. Courage, inordinate physical and spiritual resilience, and the relegation of private safety to secondary importance are recurrent themes throughout Jane's account, endowing it with an almost hagiographic aura. In this respect, the memoir resembles, and may even have been influenced by, tales of the adventurous lives of explorers and missionaries, a genre especially popular with Victorian readers. Jane's self-image emerges very clearly and is central to the narrative; she repeatedly asserts a belief in her own moral fortitude and strength of character. While not wishing to cast aspersions upon Jane's good name or imply any deliberate intention to mislead, I remain convinced that she has embellished her autobiography to reinforce and convey this obviously elevated sense of self-esteem. Of course, we can all be guilty of such innocent subjectivity when telling stories, inflating our own capacity, painting bygone troubles as just that bit more daunting to augment our triumph, in an attempt to impress the given audience. Anecdotes about devastating draughts, flying sheep, and close shaves with lightning are obviously open to exaggeration, with the power of the air current, the distance travelled by the poor beasts, and the length of Jane's unconsciousness all likely subjects for overstatement.

2. Society, community, and family

Jane Robson's life story exemplifies the gradual progress made by many of the Scottish families who settled in rural Buenos Aires Province. The pattern of Jane's existence, and that of her kin, was one of steady advance and acquisition of property, cut across by the occasional dramatic setback and resultant new beginning. After a spell in the city during the civil war of 1828 to 1829, for instance, the Rodger family returned to their rural home only to find it had been ransacked and destroyed: 'everything that would burn had gone, and there was nothing left but ashes'. Having already learned that the family had been doing well prior to the war, acquiring a partnership in a large dairy farm and even importing some pigs from home, we might expect that the loss of nearly all their hard-earned property would have proved a devastating, spirit-breaking blow. Somewhat surprisingly, Jane's account reveals no hint of a negative attitude or inclination to bow to unfortunate circumstance; on the contrary, the Rodgers simply started over again and willingly put in the hours of labour required.

Their next trial came in the form of a drought, probably the same 'gran seco' described by Charles Darwin in *The Voyage of the Beagle* (1839).[27] Jane tells us that many of her family's animals perished, again reducing them to penury. More hard work brought renewed prosperity, permitting the Rodgers to purchase a tract of land and build a better residence which they called New Caledonia, a name that clearly demonstrates the endurance of their Scottish identity. Around 1840, Jane left home to marry Hugh Robson, another Scot who had arrived in Argentina as a child on board the *Symmetry*. Many of the original settlers gathered for the

---

27. In *The Voyage of the Beagle* (London: Heron Books, 1968), Darwin notes:
    'The period between the years 1827 and 1830 is called the "gran seco," or the great drought. During this time so little rain fell, that the vegetation, even to the thistles, failed; the brooks were dried up, and the whole country assumed the appearance of a dusty high road . . . The lowest estimation of the loss of cattle in the province of Buenos Ayres alone, was taken at one million head. A proprietor at San Pedro had previously to these years 20,000 cattle; at the end not one remained' (p. 133).

ceremony, revealing the durability of ethnic bonds and their sense of solidarity. Once married, Jane's life became no easier and the routine ordeals of her youth were re-enacted. The theft of horses by passing soldiers, the misappropriation of property by creole, Irish and even Scottish neighbours, and the periodic disturbance of moving to start afresh on better lands all had to be withstood.

We have noted the bond of community which lent some coherence to the Scottish incomers as an entity, but throughout Jane Robson's account family ties take precedence and form the principal point of reference of the individual settler. In Jane's experience, the nuclear family (mother, father, plus dependent children) constituted the single most important element of social and economic organisation. The concept of family that emerges from Jane's life story extends beyond the autarkic, self-contained unit we might expect the settler in a strange land to favour, resembling instead a microcosm of liberal social organisation which functions as guardian of moral values and agent of good deeds, with altruistic tentacles spreading into the outside world. The forthcoming illustrations should clarify the point.

Despite the trying circumstances of Jane's childhood and adult life, the family units of which she was a member always displayed uncommon willingness to help fellow human beings, especially those in unfortunate circumstances. This generosity prevailed even when the actions of others might have justified a less charitable reaction. Soon after Mrs Rodger had secured shelter in the city for herself and the children during the civil war of 1828 to 1829, Jane fell ill with measles and the entire family were turned out of their lodgings by the landlady, who was anxious to protect her own offspring from contact with the infectious disease. The Rodgers' plight was aggravated by the fact that Jane's mother was herself unwell and not up to the task of finding alternative accommodation, though this necessity was finally attended to by friends. Nothing out of the ordinary so far, the reader may think, but the twist is yet to come. A short while later, Jane's mother heard that the children of the woman who evicted her had contracted smallpox, but nobody would help them, such was the terror inspired by that disease. Demonstrating absolute selflessness, Mrs Rodger went to the family's aid and nursed the children back to health. In subsequent years, the Rodgers again came to the rescue of this unfortunate family, taking them into their home after the husband's business had failed.

The Rodgers' generosity is further demonstrated by the fact that the family provided shelter, sustenance, and education for no less than seven orphan boys. When narrating this episode, Jane adds: 'at that time slavery had not been suppressed, and in some instances great cruelty took place, so that when kind people took and cared for these homeless little creatures, it was a great blessing for them'. Notwithstanding her reference to cruelty, Jane saw nothing wrong in resorting to strong measures to keep the boys in check, mentioning that she 'had a whip, and used it too'.

Once an adult, Jane continued the tradition of charity established by her parents. At one point she provided refuge to a man who was fleeing to avoid conscription into the army. This deed was to pay unexpected dividends some years later. Around 1853, we are told, the Robsons took in a man, his pregnant wife and child, and Jane even nursed the woman through labour. One day, after the family had been with them for about six months, Jane and her husband went to the market in Chascomús, leaving their youngest child in his cradle and the older children playing outside. On their way home from town, the Robsons observed a pall of smoke hanging over their property; it transpired that their guests had stolen a considerable amount of money concealed in the house, set the building alight, and escaped. Jane's baby would have been burnt alive in his crib had it not been for a passer-by who, in the course of attempting to extinguish the blaze, had discovered the child. By some amazing coincidence, the Good Samaritan was the same man whom Jane had earlier helped to elude the military.

3. Religion

Like most of their fellow Scottish settlers, the Robson family enjoyed an active and enduring involvement in the Presbyterian churches established by the community in Buenos Aires Province. Their name appears regularly throughout the records reproduced by James Dodds, both as generous subscribers to appeal funds and as frequent participants in the governing committees of their places of worship. Jane herself makes only passing reference to matters of religion, but these are sufficient to reveal her profound faith and the comfort she found in it. Of course, even the title of Jane's memoirs, 'Faith Hard Tried', provides some indication that religious belief was a key constituent of her personal identity. On one occasion, having fallen from her horse whilst pregnant, Jane fell 'very, very ill'. Her husband left to get help, but, in the interval, Jane's baby arrived stillborn or died soon after the birth. Alone in this desperate situation, with only the company of her other small child, Jane understandably turned to the Lord for consolation:

> With my little dead baby beside me, I made a vow to my God
> that if I were spared to do so, I would go to any woman in a
> similar situation, never mind who it was or how far away. I
> have kept that vow and many are the times that I have been
> called upon to fulfil it. In those undertakings I have always
> asked my God to be with me and help me, and I know he has,
> as I have often felt that he was very close to me.

Jane was also quick to offer thanks to God when saved from some crisis or dilemma. When her ungrateful house guests robbed her and set fire to her home, Jane's first thought on learning that her baby had been rescued from the conflagration was to direct gratitude to the Almighty, consciously suppressing the natural impulse to think only of her child and the benevolence of the passer-by. Having grabbed her infant from his saviour, she 'reverently thanked [her] God from a heart full of gratitude that he had spared [her] baby'.

With regard to the more material aspects of religion, Jane briefly tells us of the establishment of the Scots church at Chascomús, a development in which she seems to have played some personal part, probably in common with most members of the Scottish community in the district. She reveals the characteristic determination of the settlers by hinting at the sacrifices they had to make to secure their own church and stressing their resolve to reach the new building in adverse weather conditions in time for its opening ceremony:

> In 1857, our Church, St. Andrew's, was opened by the Rev. J.
> Smith D.D. It was very wet and had been so for many days
> previously; the camp was in a very bad state for driving. We had a
> large carriage and a great many of us went, but at times it seemed
> doubtful if we would manage to get to the Church at all. We had
> nine leagues to travel, *pantanos* [marshy areas] to cross, and
> sometimes it seemed impossible for us to proceed, even with the
> many strong horses we had. However, with patience and much
> bumping and rough tossings, we at last arrived. It was worth the

trouble, as we were one and all interested in the ceremony we had come to witness, for at last we had our Church. It had cost us some trouble, I suppose, and we all had in one way or another to deny ourselves something. I think we all felt it was worth it on this day, when our Church was completed, and we had met to rejoice, and knew it was a good work well done.

St Andrew's, built during the winter of 1857, became known as the Rancho Kirk, on account of the building's modest construction.[28] According to Dodds, it 'was a lowly thatched cottage, with smoothly plastered, white-washed walls, with brick paved floor, and well lighted by three windows on each side' (p. 271). Jane's allusion to the sacrifices required to finance its construction is confirmed in Dodds's account, where he records that in order to accumulate sufficient funds, every settler who owned sheep agreed to 'pay annually the value of ten sheep per thousand of their possessions' (p. 271). He claims that this unconventional method proved successful, for within a few years 'a goodly sum was soon deposited in the Provincial Bank of Chascomús' (p. 271). Dodds also gives further details of the difficulties encountered in executing the church's opening ceremony, emphasising the persevering, dauntless spirit of the Scots community and their clergyman:

> Preparations had been made for opening the church for public worship on the second Sunday of November 1857, but the weather proved unfavourable, for it rained almost incessantly for two days. We can remember the Rev. Smith's arrival (on Saturday) at Adela on horseback, amidst the driving rain, after a ride of twenty-four leagues, from the Estancia Viamont, accompanied by a guide, and clad in the picturesque uniform of oilskin and sou'-wester, supplied by Mr. Henry Bell, his kind host, who had failed to dissuade him from undertaking the journey on such a day. It rained all Sunday, and the opening of the church took place on Monday, with a fairly good congregation, as all the people knew that 'no Sunday shower ever kept Mr. Smith at home in that important hour'. (p. 272)

28. In Latin American Spanish, a 'rancho' is a hut or a shack. Only in Mexico is it commonly equivalent to the English 'ranch'.

4. Politics, the legal system, and gender discrimination
Specific references to national politics do not abound in Jane Robson's
life story, but there are a handful which merit attention. Early in her tale,
Jane recalls the civil war of 1828 to 1829 and the disruption it brought to
her childhood. Her description leaves little doubt as to the gravity of the
situation and summarises the circumstances which forced the Monte
Grande colonists to disband their settlement and flee:

> At this time the country was more and more unsettled. Rosas
> was outside, and Lavalle in, Buenos Aires. There were bands of
> Indians wandering about who were Rosas's men. Lavalle's
> soldiers were also wandering about, stealing, murdering and
> causing the greatest alarm. It was well named 'The Reign of
> Terror'. It became so terrible that all the families who possibly
> could went into the town for more safety.[29]

Jane then goes on to relate the story of the assault upon the Rodger
property by the band of brutal Rosistas who killed the family's dog.
    The next mention of Jane's life being significantly affected by political
affairs consists of a passing reference to an uprising in the south of the
Province, in which *estancieros* who had loyally supported the regime in the
past rebelled against Rosas in protest at the economic hardships resulting
from the French naval blockade of Buenos Aires between 1838 and 1840.
This group of landowners, which included a younger brother of the
dictator, Gervasio Rosas, believed that only a change of government
could bring reconciliation with France and a peaceful end to the crisis. It
would seem that some lapse of memory enters Jane's account at this point,
for her words imply that the uprising took place either during 1840 or at
some later time. This can be deduced from the fact that she has already
asserted that 1840 was the year of her marriage to Hugh Robson, and yet
she had clearly wed her husband by the outbreak of the southern
revolution:

29. It is curious that Jane describes this era as 'The Reign of Terror', for the term
    is more commonly encountered in relation to the period around 1840, when
    the Rosas regime's oppression of dissident elements reached its most intense
    phase. Perhaps she has unwittingly muddled these two episodes of unrest;
    alternatively, it is quite possible that this apt expression was in current use
    during the late 1820s and was simply revived in association with later events.

The country at this time was again very unsettled, and a revolution broke out in Chascomús, so all the English speaking people went into the city, amongst them my husband's relatives. They tried to persuade me to go also, but I said, 'No, I will remain with my husband and help him, if we must flee, we will go together'.

We know, however, that the rebellion was put down in November 1839, a fact that can be verified in any history of the period. What, then, does Jane's confusion mean? Whilst we may not expect her to be mistaken about the date of her marriage, this is the only logical explanation of the discrepancy, unless, of course, her words refer to another minor disturbance following the main uprising and neglected in historical accounts. The latter scenario is barely plausible, so we must sensibly attribute Jane's forgetfulness to the fogginess of memory brought on by her advanced age.

In addition to the anxiety brought by politically motivated agitation, Jane had to endure the direct financial ramifications of Rosas's quarrels with foreign powers. The Anglo-French naval blockade of Buenos Aires during the mid-1840s served only to make her already difficult life worse to bear, as the purchasing power of her hard-earned cash diminished. The European intervention could not have come at a less propitious time for the Robsons, as they were already wearied by a recent move:

> In 1843 we came to 'Los Sauces' . . . where we had 21,000 sheep on thirds and also a large dairy. My life seems to be made up of fresh starts after failures; it wanted a strong heart to battle with it. I had to work night and day, for at night there were the animals to look after and collect, housework, sewing and washing to do, for I had no woman to help me. We had, of course, peones for the outside work, but they were so untrustworthy and would go off on a drinking bout or amuse themselves in their own fashion and were so much trouble to look after, that they were worse than useless.

> This period was the time of the French and English blockade, and all imported things were at fabulous prices, indeed, all living was very expensive, tea at 10 dollars a pound, salt 6 dollars a

pound. This made it very difficult for us to make ends meet, though I worked as perhaps no woman has ever done – I even killed animals for our meat.

Once again, therefore, we encounter the recurrent theme of Jane's heroic struggle against adverse circumstances and we are introduced to her view of the idle disposition of the typical Argentinian.

If we broaden our definition of the political realm to include not only major events of national importance, but also the workings of local government and the administration of justice, then Jane's account becomes rather more eloquent. She relates several episodes in which the figure of the *alcalde* (the representative of the law in the area) appears, each one of which reveals Jane's belief in fair play and her desire to see justice done, values that often leave her despairing of the bias and incompetence displayed by the local officer. On only one occasion does the *alcalde* seem to have reached the right decision and meted out due punishment to a criminal, the drunken Irishman who almost killed one of Jane's neighbours in a vicious assault: 'The *alcalde* came and took the man to prison, and I heard that after a term of prison he was sent on to a ship; no doubt he was kept in order there, and trained'. Every other instance of Jane's involvement with the law proves unsatisfactory. In 1860, we are told, she forcibly apprehended a neighbour who had been stealing her family's animals, but the representative of justice 'simply let him go free'. At another time, Jane rescued a badly injured Irishman from a knife fight, only to have to make further efforts to save him from undeserved arrest:

> I bound his wounded hand up in my large neck handkerchief and rode off with him to our house. We had no sooner got in safely when I saw the *alcalde* and two soldiers coming. I went to the door and stood with a hand on either side waiting for them. They came with much bluster and said they had come for the man and would take him away bound like a pig. I said, 'You will not have him and don't dare to put a foot in my house. The man is seriously wounded; if you took him and he died, his death would be at your door. I will be responsible for him appearing before the Justice'.

Having undermined the authority of the *alcalde* in the presence of his underlings, Jane added to the affront by presenting her version of the case to the judge before the *alcalde* received his hearing, with the result that her wounded charge was set free. It would appear that there was no guarantee of impartiality within the Argentine legal system at this time, for the offended officer simply turned his position into an instrument of revenge: 'The *alcalde* was furious, and after this he never lost a chance of doing us harm if he could'. Presumably, his hostility was just another of the many obstacles which Jane and her family had to face on a daily basis.

The slow pace of the legal process was a further irritation to the Robsons, specifically when Jane required the signature of the local judge upon a document. Frustrated by a long delay in the completion of this simple task, Jane set out to resolve the matter in her own fashion, presenting herself in person before the magistrate. In doing so, Jane defied a tradition that she regarded as absurd, namely that women were excluded from the inner sanctum of the law offices. Rather than peaceably accepting this barrier, she rebelled against the norm, burst into the judge's room, demanded his immediate attention, and finally achieved her objective.

On another occasion, Jane's bold resistance to prejudice against women seems to have brought a permanent change of policy. While nursing a sick acquaintance, identified only as Mrs R., Jane decided that her patient required better medical attention than that provided by the local doctor, whose opinion was that 'if her bodily health improved, her mind would never be strong again'. To this end, she decided to transport the poor woman to the British Hospital in Buenos Aires, an institution which still exists today. Having reached the hospital, Jane had to struggle to persuade the doctor in charge to violate established protocol and accept a female patient, but, in doing so, she appears to have set a precedent for the future:

> I went in first, and to my astonishment and disgust the Doctor informed me the hospital was not for women but only for men, and that he could not receive Mrs R. I said he must, or I would tell everybody that they had refused to take in a sick woman when brought to the doors of the hospital . . . The doctor then said he would take her but that it would be at his own risk, as

he did not know what unpleasantness might arise and how his action might be questioned. We took her into a room, and her sister and I remained to nurse her, for there were no women nurses and this was the first woman patient that had been taken into the British Hospital. From that time to the present both sexes were received.

As well as revealing her individual audacity, Jane's successful brow-beating of the tardy judge and the reluctant doctor serves as evidence of the settlers' ability to get things done, to act when the conventions of local society decreed passivity. The incomers' natural reluctance to be bound by ingrained customs, especially when their different outlook suggested a more efficient course of action, was a clear attribute if they were to assist in bringing the transformation of society sought by their creole proponents. Blind tolerance of old ways was not for the likes of Jane; she followed the dictates of conscience, regardless of external pressures and oblivious to the protests of others.

Editorial note

The text of William Grierson's 'The Voyage of the *Symmetry*' reproduced here is transcribed from that originally printed for the St Andrew's Presbyterian Church in Buenos Aires. This version of the journal was circulated in eight instalments as a supplement to the Church newsletter at a date I have been unable to establish definitively, although all indications are that it appeared in the early decades of the present century. To the best of my knowledge, 'Faith Hard Tried' has not appeared in print previously.[30]

In rendering these accounts for publication, alterations have been limited to those of punctuation and orthography strictly required for the sake of clarity and consistency. In the case of 'The Voyage of the *Symmetry*', I have resisted the temptation to revise Grierson's frequently unorthodox style, simply to conserve the spontaneous quality of observations jotted down briskly and without extensive premeditation. All

30. Brief introduced extracts from 'The Voyage of the *Symmetry*' and 'Faith Hard Tried' are due to appear in the forthcoming *Scottish Migration to the Americas, c. 1650-1939: A Documentary Source Book*, ed. by Allan I. Macinnes and others (Edinburgh: Pillans and Wilson, forthcoming).

elucidation of references to historical events and personages, geographical locations, and local customs, when not already covered in this Introduction, is presented in the form of footnotes. Translations of isolated Spanish words or phrases, as well as any other editorial interpolations in the main texts, are enclosed within brackets.

A number of footnotes to the Introduction and accounts contain suggestions for further reading. Wherever possible, these indicate items published in English; however, when a work in the Spanish language proves the most appropriate for citation, every effort has been made to include reference to an English alternative too.

THE VOYAGE
OF THE *SYMMETRY*
by
William Grierson

THE VOYAGE OF THE SYMMETRY

The Voyage of the Symmetry, From a Journal, of the Voyage, of the Ship Symmetry of Scarborough, Capt. Smith Master, from Leith[1] to Buenos Ayres, Between May the 20th, and Augt. the 11th inclusive, 1825, by Mr. Grierson, one of the Passengers, for the satisfaction of his friends in Scotland.

MAY, 1825

20th Being Friday, went with my family on board, the ship lying in Leith Roads, all things ready, expecting to sail by the night-tide. Found the greatest confusion, in every part, the Steerage baffles all description, Beds, Blankets, Clothes, Bales, Packages, items of every kind all in a huddle. Sailors, Passengers, Strangers, sick, healthy, old and young, sober, tipsy, crying, praying, scolding, Things serious and comic, all going on at one and the same time. This is a world of itself. We have hatch-holes; but no backdoors. If things are to continue as they begin, the sooner our voyage is at an end the better. Find the small apartment allotted to my family as tolerable (comfortable not to be expected), as any that I see: being a small Cabin-closet, containing 3 beds; 2 to be occupied by my family, and 1 by my female cousins, the two Miss Broaches.

21st Saturday, Early on deck, still riding at anchor, a fine morning, yesterday's confusion still continues, huddle, hubbub, and hurly burly as fresh as ever. Whilst at breakfast (half 8 o'clock) the Capt. observed 'that our Broker had neglected to send any baconham aboard, and he thought we should remind him of it', accordingly, as the Capt. was going ashore, I, for one, went along with him, and caused Mr. Broadfoot (our Broker) to send us 24 good hams for the Cabin, these will be very serviceable. While, on the pier, seeking out a boat to return aboard, I met with Miss

---

1. *Leith*: the port of Edinburgh, in the River Forth.

41

Marion Kelton, and one of Miss Montgomerie's servt. girls. They brought me 3 letters from Waterfoot, went on Board, and sent a line on shore, to Miss Montgomerie. Mr. Broadfoot (our Broker) came aboard, and then there was a hurry in the Steerage, getting all things put to rights. Our Employer's Father and Mother paid us a visit today: We had an excellent dinner, it was soon observable that the old gentleman was no novice in the Mysteries of Bacchus, and the old Dame felt so comfortable among us, that she refused to go ashore, and declared 'that she was determined to go to Buenos Ayres': and at last, we found it necessary to chair her, much agt. her will, and heave her, with all due respect, into the boat. Our Brick layers, from London, seemed determined to find fault with every thing, and one of them got to cuffs, with one of our Scotch lads; but he had much better have let it alone, as the Scotchman beat him most completely, and hurt him very much. Our worthy Capt. at last interfered, and declared in the most positive terms 'that he would put into Irons the first man, that should offer at such things in future.' It is to be hoped this will have a salutary effect on John Bull. I walked on the Deck till about mid-night, and the Capt. and I could not but express our mutual regret, to see the Steerage so much crowded, and so much human misery. This has been a fine day, wind Easterly.

22nd Sabbath. Early on deck. Under full sail, a perfect calm. Slip gently along with the Ebb, drop anchor about noon. A gentle breeze arises about 4 p.m. weigh anchor. The Pilot leaves us about this time. Send a line ashore to Miss Montgomerie. Passengers appear to be getting happy. The confusion much subsided, almost no sickness. The English and Scotch seem to be getting more friendly with one another. A smart shower about 5 p.m. The calm continues all day. No view, the air being foggy. Make small progress. Elements!! Have ye conspired to give us a silent farewell? The Sun is dim; the air is dead; and not a purl can be seen, not a Dimple on the serene face of the Forth: from whose bosom we are now gently gliding, perhaps, ere long, to become the sport of the Ocean. Ye misty banks, ye foggy hills, ye cloud covered mountains of our country, have you arrayed yourselves in your sable weeds, out of compliment to our feelings; for sure the strongest links of friendship's chain riveted in our hearts are upon the rack? Must we bid you adieu? We will bear you in our Breasts. We will look to the South. We will court your forms in distant climes. Our present children will prattle your names, and our future offspring shall learn your songs. When we have passed the Sun, when we have found what we may call a new heaven and a new earth, we will hold you in remembrance, and a third part of Earth's circumference shall not separate you from us, even when there (if ever we get there) our friendship shall operate; our mutual correspondence will demonstrate that our reciprocal *Love* is immortal. But I must not indulge, such reveries, however delightful, may all end in illusion, it is now 10 at night and we are all abed.

23 – Monday – reach the deck about 8 a.m. a foggy morning – observe a number of Vessels on the same course with ourselves – we are leaving them very fast. – Surely the Symmetry is a fine Sailer – not one of all these can come near us – the English coast appears, at a distance – Wind N.E. the Capt. says we must go South about. Catharine and the Children quite well, and in high spirits – a wet day at 2 p.m. – an excellent dinner at ½-3, nothing need be better. – Tea at ½-6. Grog at 9. – Supper and to bed – this afternoon the Lads and Lasses had a merry dance on deck. One of the Dairy-Maids happened to miss a foot; she tumbled down stairs, and, poor thing, got herself considerably bruised. – Surely the Seafaring life is full of variety, and the human disposition, under its influence becomes as changeable as the weather – for these poor creatures, who appeared dying on Saturday, are dancing mad, on Monday – this day may be termed dull and foggy, little land to be seen.

24th Tuesday. – Get upon deck a little after 5 – a close dull morning. – wind right ahead, from the South hard upon the rocky Yorkshire coast – it appeared very awful, as the waves were dashing – with all their might upon the rocks, raising the spray very high, and covering all the shore with foam – now we make a tack for the first time, and beat to windward. the ship rolls and jumps like a cork. Most of our merry last-night's dancers, and many more, now are sick, and emptying their Breadbaskets most completely. in place of 44, only 10, besides little Willie and myself, found the way to the Breakfast-table about ½ past 8. – after Breakfast the day mends. – got our lunch about 12, off Scarborough,[2] the air dead

2. *Scarborough*: port and seaside resort in North Yorkshire, located some 36 miles north-east of York.

calm, the sea swelling, mightily. – a short thunder shower, with a light squall, and then a dead calm. – all hands in motion another squall, during which, nothing to be heard, but the rattling of sails, and crashing of cordage: and then a calm.

We pass Robinhood's bay, and the calm continues till we go to bed.

25th Wednesday. – A squally morning, after the most disagreeable night that I ever passed; the calm continued throughout the whole night: the swell being very strong, the Vessel kept bobbing like a buoy: nothing to be heard but sick passengers crying to be set ashore; – all a dying – wind S by W. Tack close in upon the shore, exactly opposite Hamborough-head,[3] which has, indeed, a most Majestic appearance. It Blew very hard. Our Breakfast-ranks very thin, this morning. Feel not the least effects upon myself. My appetite never was better. It cleared up, and the Capt. ordered a general muster, about 11 a.m. upon deck, with Beds to be aired. This was the most wonderful turn out that I ever beheld. I never expected to have seen so many sick folk in one place. It is surely an hospital: – However it had a very good effect, and they seemed much benefited by it. Catharine and the Children, who had been a little sick, now got quite well. – after Dinner (at 3) went upon deck and counted 56 sail in view, wind veered to N.E. – Tea at 6. a fine breeze. – hope to get forward. – sailing at the rate of 6 knots an hour. – bed at 9. – a fine night, after a showery day with some thunder. –

26th Thursday. – A fine morning about 7 – wind fair, from the N. upwards of 40 sail in view; we keep the lead, not one can come up with us. – we pass many of them. – sailing along the Norfolk coast. We arrive at Yarmouth roads.[4] – Send a letter to my Father, by a boat that happened to pass us. – count 100 sail all in view. – running at the rate of 7 miles an hour, – write 2 letters more, one for Miss Montgomerie and one for Mrs. Kelton: but had not an opportunity of putting them ashore. – All well. – the wind fair from the N. going on fine. – to bed about ½ 9. –

3. *Hamboroughhead*: Grierson must mean Flamborough Head, a rocky promontory in the former East Riding of Yorkshire (now part of Humberside). Perhaps this misspelling arises from 'Fl' being read as 'H' when the original manuscript was transcribed.

4. (Great) *Yarmouth*: port and seaside resort at the mouth of the River Yare in the county of Norfolk, some 110 miles north-east of London.

27th Friday. – Mount Deck about 6 a very wet blowy morning; – wind fair. – we had passed the Downs,[5] and Straits of Dover,[6] during the night. – right opposite Beachy Head.[7] – the Chalky Sussex-shore full in view, white as snow. – smart Breeze, and rough sea. – many sick. – running 8 Knots an hour. about 11 a.m. the Isle of Wight made its appearance; we passed it about 3 p.m. – Our Londoners, who had been pretty quiet, ever since we left the Forth, would not have cared to mutiny, to day, about their grog. – But our worthy Sovereign (Capt. S.) plainly told them, 'that he would give grog to those to whom grog did good, that is, to the sober, and peace-able; but that nothing was as suitable for fractious dispositions as fetters, and these should be applied, whenever they appeared neces-sary'. – And to this our London lads were obliged to say amen. – about ½-4 p.m. St. Alban's Head[8] came in view, and running pretty quick, with a fair Wind from N.E. we passed it (St. Alban's Head) at 8 in the evening; and now the steady, and revolving lights of Portland[9] guide our course. – this is a fine evening; but our wind begins to fail.

28th Saturday. – A fine morning; wind right ahead nearly due W. – all well. – a fine day. – make nothing of it. – just plying away opposite Portland, the winds seem as if they were determined to detain us in the Channel: stop us not, we are resolved upon going. – our address to you when we left the Forth, we need not recapitulate. –

29th Sabbath. – A fine morning, wind steady; and right ahead. Start point[10] in view, about 10 a.m., tacking up and down. – Mr. Fisher, at the desire of the Capt. gave us Prayers, upon deck. We had a full turn out, and nothing, but silence and attention. I never, at any time in my life, nor in any place, or on any occasion, saw so solemn an assembly – had a pin

5. (South) *Downs*: low-lying coastal hills, mainly employed as pasture land, in the southern English counties of Hampshire and Sussex.
6. *Straits of Dover*: major shipping lane connecting the North Sea and the English Channel.
7. *Beachy Head*: promontory on the south coast of England, near Eastbourne, in the county of East Sussex.
8. *St. Alban's Head*: promontory on the south coast of England, in the county of Dorset, between Durlston Head and Portland (see note 9).
9. (Isle of) *Portland*: a rocky limestone peninsula on the south coast of England, in the county of Dorset.
10. *Start point*: a headland to the south-west of Torquay, in the county of Devon.

dropped upon deck, it would have been heard from the one end of the ship to the other. It may be affirmed that to all appearance, none of us, ever attended to the duties of devotion with more sincerity, or joined in prayer more fervently. Nor could any preparation of man have been better adopted, to fit us for religious adoration, than the circumstances in which we were placed. – nor could any other employment be more suitable for our present situation, than that, wherein we were engaged. – The whole of this day was spent in a religious manner. – in reading, in listening, and serious conversation. I never witnessed less levity on any Sabbath. And our worthy Capt. was exemplary in every thing. – it may be said of him, that he laid down his regulations, in every respect, with the soundest wisdom, and conformed to them himself, and caused others to observe them, with the nicest punctuality. He keeps his hours upon Deck, by night, and day, the very same as the lowest man upon Watch, – he sees every thing is in every place, and always where he should be. – He is the most polite, sober, pleasant and agreeable man that I ever was in company with. – Nor does he appear more indebted, for his eminence, to his acquired talents than to the natural dispositions of his heart. – in a word, I think he is a good man, and wishes all around him to be good and happy. – He seems very partial to me, and will do anything in his power to promote my comfort, or that of my family: and when at Table, he either is, or I suppose him to be, best pleased, when I support him on the right: a place which I frequently occupy. I have scarcely heard an oath since I came on board. Our punishment for profane swearing is immediate excommunication; we will not so much as look upon the man, who may aim at it and I do not believe that Britain can produce such a Capt. for regularity in all respects. We pass start point about 4 p.m., the wind more favourable; sailing due West, the Capt. says this will be the last British land that we will see, if the wind hold: – getting finely on. – the wind still favourable. – it has been a fine day with a shower at night. –

30th Monday. – Take a Dose of Salts: feel the Ship rocking pretty much. – rise at 6. – no Land in view. – running straight for the Bay of Biscay, which we enter about 4 p.m. – 3 sail in view – our rate today was about 8½ Knots an hour. – the wind right N. a very fine day. –

31st Tuesday. – A fine morning, in the Bay of Biscay – wind fair; but very little of it. – our rate from 3 to 4 miles an hour. Our Longitude to day 8.55 W. a very pleasant day, and we amuse ourselves in playing at Pitchin with Coppers about 9 p.m., we observe a sail on the same tract with ourselves. A most delightful night, the sea perfectly smooth the Moon, being full, had a most beautiful disk, when viewed through the Telescope. the evening feels warm.

JUNE, 1825

1st Wednesday. – A fine morning, with a scantling of wind from the S.W., and a very smooth sea, though in the Bay of Biscay. It is all nonsense about the Sea's being rougher here than elsewhere: the Capt., says it depends entirely upon the weather; we have not had so level water, since we left Leith roads. The Capt., ordered Mr. Galbrath and me, to inspect the Steerage, and see, that all the Hammocks were clean. – we found a number of them not in very good condition all were ordered on Deck, and we caused every berth to be washed out, and Hair-Combs to be applied, to prevent the increase of small Cattle,[11] which we found in some cases were beginning to multiply: henceforth the Steerage to be daily examined, by two, from the Cabin, alternately; and in case any casualties of the above description appeared in future, they were to be exposed upon deck; and personal cleanliness was to be the watchword. – at 4 p.m. a smart breeze struck up, which increased till 10. this was a fine day; but it now appears squally. – to bed at 10. –

2nd. – Thursday – a squally morning; went on deck as early as 3. – sea running mountain high – glad to creep into bed again: – rose at ½-6 – sea still rougher, and rising higher. – all sick, my family excepted. – I felt a little squeamish; but it went off after Breakfast. – during Breakfast, we could use neither Table, nor properly dishes: we could not keep upon our seats; every thing at liberty was tossed topsy-turvy. – the tempest increasing, one sail was hauled down down down after another, until

11. *small Cattle*: a euphemistic description of head lice, common in some dialects of Scots.

we had only one square sail, and two small treble-reefed topsails standing – the Ladies got an awful fright: – I confess that I could have formed no Idea of such a scene. – about 3 p.m. it began to rain, with a tremendous blast; and after a little time, we had a dead calm, – not a breath of air: the swell continued, mighty indeed: – this was worse than all that had been, and we had to cling to whatever fixture we could lay hold of – in a little a fresh squall, with a change of wind. – at 5, a hurricane, with rain, and 'all Sails down', was the order. – So much for the B.[ay] of B.[iscay] and such we found it. – both calm and tempestuous. – this squall was of short duration, and then the wind became fair: but the swell continued. – Dinner ranks very thin – only two Ladies – Catharine being one of them – the Capt. and other 3 gentlemen, alongst with myself. – All the rest quite sick. – I said to myself, this is surely the climax of our distress; I never saw, I hope I never will again behold, the like of this. – at 9 p.m. wind fair, running 5 miles an hour. This has been a dreadful day in the Bay of Biscay.

3rd – Friday – Fine morning. – fair wind: but very rough swell. – rate 6 miles an hour. – many sick. – my family all well. – The servts. in the steerage complain that the Cooks were dirty. – the Capt. caused the pottage to be inspected: we found it to be unfit for human use: – Orders were given to have the Cooks (two of our Londoners) tied to the windlass, and severely flogged – But as they were very fervent in their deprecations, and seemed serious in promises of amendment; alleging in extenuation of their guilt; 'that as the Sea had been so rough, for some time past, they could not get *them* coppers scoured': – they were pardoned, at this time; but our worthy Capt. told them plainly, 'that if he heard a complaint of the same kind, in future, their shoulders should feel all the virtue of a rope's-end.' – Our little sow farrowed last night: the litter consists of 16, all doing well. – our rate throughout this day about 6 Knots an hour. – Lat. 44.55 – Long: 11.46. this has been a fine warm day.

4th. – Saturday. – Get on Deck at 6, steady breeze from S.W. – going on finely. – Top sail ahead in view, – we came up to it about 10 a.m. Capt. spoke her through the Trumpet, after *we* had hoisted English, and *they* Swedish colours. they were from Norway, bound for Lisbon. – we were all upon deck, passed her in grand style, giving three cheers, which they, after taking off their caps, politely returned. – this was a high treat for us; but in a very short time we lost sight of them. – Lat: today about 42. – we had passed cape Finisterre;[12] and were now opposite Vigo,[13] a port of Spain, in Galicia. – rate of sailing 6 or 7 knots. – and a fine day. –

5th. – Sabbath – A fine morning, but dull. – at 10 a.m. all on deck; Mr. Fisher reads prayers, after the English form, and one of Blair's sermons. – every thing went on with the greatest solemnity; more so than I have sometimes seen in one of our Churches: and the remainder of the day was spent like last Sabbath. – in religious reading, and pious conversations. – in the evening much fish, of the Porpois-Kind made its appearance. – they came very close to the ship, in great numbers, so that we had a full view of them: they were shaped, in some respects, not unlike our salmon: cut very large, and otherwise very different from any thing that I had ever seen. – One of the sailors caught a Turtle-dove, upon deck, which had followed us for two days. it was put into a cage. – it is a beautiful little bird, not so large as a pigeon. – its colour much like a Jay-Pyet. – the days are now getting shorter, and very warm: quite mild at night. Lat. 40. – wind fair; but very scanty.

6th. Monday – a very dull, mild calm morning – going at 3 miles an hour. – at 3 a.m. opposite Lisbon. we expect to see the Madeiras[14] by tomorrow evening. at 7 p.m. a fine breeze – going 7 miles an hour. Lat: 37. warm Thermometer in the shade 66. –

7th. Tuesday – A fine morning. – feel very unwell. – can take no victuals all day: rather alarmed; my pulse about 100 per minute. – The Dr. imputes it to the sudden change of climate, and gives me a smart dose of Physic, which has a good effect. – much fish along side to day. – they speared one about 40 lb. wt. I think they call it the Albecor. – wind fair; but scant. – only 3 or 4 Knots. – Running right for the Madeiras. Lat. 35.49. the Ther: in the shade about 70. –

12. *cape Finisterre*: a rocky headland in Galicia, in north-west Spain, the westernmost point of the Spanish mainland.
13. *Vigo*: Atlantic port and resort about 10 miles north of the Portuguese border.
14. *Madeiras*: group of volcanic islands belonging to Portugal, lying in the Atlantic some 560 miles south-west of Lisbon.

8th. Wednesday. – Got upon deck about 7 a.m. a fine morning – feel much better; but not well. – they had taken another fish. – some of it cooked for breakfast. – it was generally relished. – I tasted it and thought it good. – wind steady; but very little of it. – There has scarcely been a sail to alter during the last 3 days. – we got up our awning today, and found much benefit from it. – Lat. 34.25. – Ther: in the shade 72. feels very warm.–

9th. Thursday. – Mount deck about 6 a.m. Porto Santo[15] nearly opposite, distant about 2 leagues. – a fine morning. – The East end of the Island reminds me much of Arthur's seat, and Salisbury Craig.[16] – there are 4, or 5 rocky eminencies upon it, one of which considerably out-tops the rest; they appear very majestic when viewed through the Glass. – it seems very barren. – we are now beginning to have a faint view of Madeira. – caught two more fishes. – I relish them much; never found anything finer. – and they seem to be light upon the stomach. – we are now all well, thanks to *God* for it. – about 12 noon, we are right opposite Madeira, being to the N.E. of it. – It appears mountainous, with summits almost piercing the Clouds. – and the shore seems rocky, and nothing but Crags. – Still it is the house of Bacchus, and its Breweries diffuse their genial qualities around this Globe. – I have two letters ready to send home; but no opportunity of putting them ashore. – we throw three sealed Bottles into the Sea, which, should they reach the hands of Man, may tell who, and where we are. – Towards evening we pass the Island in grand style. – no shipping to be seen. – a fine day, and fair breeze, rate 6 Knots: and the Ther: 91 in the shade.

10th. Friday. – A dull morning; a sharp, fresh, steady, fair breeze, which continues through the day. – we get finely on 7 ½ Knots. Lat. 31.21, all well. – Ther: 70 in the shade. – Heat not felt so oppressive owing to the Breeze.

11th. Saturday. – A fine morning. – Wind as yesterday. – the rays of the sun very warm. – Lat: 29. – Ther: in the shade 72. – rate 6 Knots. – it now feels very warm in the Evenings. –

15. *Porto Santo*: the second largest of the Madeira islands.
16. *Arthur's seat*: the 823 ft hill which overlooks the city of Edinburgh; *Salisbury Craig* (or Crag) is a cliff on the same volcanic mass.

12th. Sabbath. – A pleasant morning. – Breeze light, and fair. – sailing 5 miles an hour. – got on deck after breakfast. – observe the flying fish, for the first time: they appear to be about 4 inches long. – rise out of the water just like a flock of birds on a winter day, and continue on the wing, for the distance of 15, or 20 yards. – at ½ 10, we had prayers, and a sermon; and observed the Sabbath, in our usual solemn manner. – at Dinner a misunderstanding, between the Capt. and Mr. Fisher took place, for which we are all very sorry; as it does not appear to be easily made up, and the Capt. declares that he will not sit at table with him. I am afraid lest this should hurt our society, and throw us into party work. – This has been fine day; but warm. – Lat: 27.1. – Ther: 73. –

13th. Monday. – A fine warm morning. – Breeze light, and fair. – going at 3 miles an hour; Lat: 25.29. Ther: 75 in the shade. – The Capt. does not sit with us owing to yesterday's misunderstanding with Mr. Fisher, which seems not easily to be made up. feels very warm. –

14th. Tuesday. – A fine morning: very warm. – a Sail ahead, on the same course with us. – The Cooks threaten to give up their office, unless they get some assistance; we got one to help them, and they appeared satisfied. – Breeze light: but fair. – about 5 p.m. hailed a French Brig: but rec'd in return, 'that they could not speak no Anglee Inglish'. – We passed her in fine style, with our Bagpipe playing. – our Water now very bad. – even when made into Tea, it smells strong. – our allowance of Porter[17] is very agreeable – but for it we would be ill – did not go to bed till 12 midnight, could not keep below, owing to the heat. – Sun nearly vertical: the Lat. about 23. Ther: 80, in the shade. – very warm; perspiring at every pore, most copiously.

15th – Wednesday. – Fine morning – a smart fresh breeze. – not so sultry to day. – The Ladies mostly all complaining. – The Dr. thinks yesterday's heat has overcome them. – Catharine had a touch of the headach; but it soon went off. – plenty of small flying fish. – *a vertical sun* – very warm. – we will continue our awning until we reach a colder climate: – being the most of our time on deck. – we perspire freely, during the coolest part of

17. *Porter:* a dark, bitter beer brewed from charred or browned malt.

the night, when under nothing but a single sheet: nay even when uncovered altogether, and we never go to bed till about midnight. – Lat: 22.5. Ther: 76 in the shade. – rate of sailing 5 ½ Knots. – we now enjoy the Tradewind[18] perfectly steady – not a sail to alter. The Heavens are most brilliant, at night; and the N.pole is creeping towards the Horizons, and we have had no rain for sometime back; – it is clear delightful weather, only a shade too warm, and very sultry at nights.

16th. – Thursday – reach the deck about 5 a.m. found it very sultry below; – a fine fresh breeze, pleasant morning – running at the rate of 5 miles an hour. – plenty of flying fish. – they appear very beautiful, clear as silver. – They start up every now, and then, like a flock of pigeons. – we expect to see the cape Verde[19] by tomorrow evening, if this breeze continues. – Many very sick. – Lat: 20.8. – Ther: about 80, rate 6 miles an hour.

17th. – Friday. – Mount deck about 6. – a fine morning. – nice light breeze. – Still a number sick, about 4 p.m. got a faint, and distant view of the Cape Verde. – at 2 p.m. a sail to the E. – did not come near each other. – To day about 5 p.m. Our London gentry squabbled with the Sailors: but here also, the Cockneys were foiled, and 2, or 3 of them got a most complete drubbing, which they richly deserved, and which, it is to be hoped will keep them quiet during the remainder of the Voyage. – Lat: 18.2 – Ther: in the shade 75. – rate 5 ½ Knots. – bed about 12. –

18th – Saturday – A warm morning, and light breeze – pass the Cape Verds.[20] – about noon, almost a dead calm: and anything exposed to the sun's rays could scarcely be touched by the hand, being so very hot. – A shark, the first we had seen, made his appearance; he followed us a long way; made several attempts at a piece of Beef, hung out to steep; at last one of the Sailors drove an harpoon into him, which held for some time;

18. *Tradewind*: the so-called trade winds blow steadily towards the equator from the north-east in the northern hemisphere and from the south-east in the southern hemisphere.

19. *cape Verde*: Atlantic peninsula between the Senegal and Gambia rivers, mainland Africa's most westerly point.

20. *Cape Verds* (or Cape Verdes): formerly a Portuguese colony, now an independent island republic, lying in the Atlantic off the coast of Senegal.

but he got free at length and made off – we got a full view of him, as he came boldly up close along side; an ugly looking creature, resembling what we commonly call an Arsk; has to turn on his back when he bites, on account of his upper jaw being prominent. – he seemed to be about 6 feet long: – the Capt. says he is only a young one and not half the size of what he has seen them. – This is the warmest day we have had; when wanting, both Neck-Cloth, and Coat, we perspired profusely. – about 2 p.m. a breeze struck up suddenly, and we went on briskly. – At 4 p.m., the cloth being laid in both Cabins, the Gentlemen were ordered to the after Cabin, as Mrs. Aird claimed an exclusive privilege to the fore one; and before we had finished our Dinner, word was sent in, 'that she was safely delivered of a fine Daughter, both doing well'. – this makes the 212th passenger. – this being Waterloo-anniversary,[21] we indulged in an extra Glass, on that account, and to Mrs. Aird's safe recovery, with a welcome to our young passenger. – Moreover, every Saturday-night, we have a toast to all absent friends, and we think on the land of Cakes.[22] – A great number sick, owing to the heat and crowded state of the Vessel. – Lat: 16.20. – Ther. 80 in the shade. – running in the after noon about 8, or 9 Knots.

19th. – Sabbath. – A Boisterous morning. – side-wind. – the storm increases, as the day advances. – the sea often breaking over the deck. – many sick. – my family all well, thank *God*, for it. – Mrs. Aird, and child doing well. – many of the passengers have had a sorry time of it. – whenever the sea gets rough, they become sick as ever. – have no public worship today, on account of the storm. – The Mate observed that he had never seen such a squall, in these Latitudes, at any former period. towards evening the breeze calms; and then it becomes very sultry. – one of the Sailors gets a severe cut on the head, by a Block falling upon it, occasioned by a rope giving way. – we all think the poor fellow has left us: the Dr. thinks not. – the Capt. shaved his head, the Dr. dressed the wound, and we rejoice to see him still alive. – Plenty of air; but hot as if from a furnace. – Lat: 13:44. Ther. 78. – rate 6 Knots. –

21. The Battle of Waterloo, in which Napoleon's army was defeated by the
    Duke of Wellington's forces, took place on 18 June 1815.
22. *land of Cakes*: a fond nickname for Scotland.

20th. – Monday. – a fine morning; but warm, after an almost intolerable night. – though the hatches were open, with Airbags at each; it was with difficulty that we breathed below. – Catharine unwell during the night, but gets better, so soon as she got into the fresh air. – we had a full turnout to day: the sick amounted to nearly one-half. – the Steerage all washed out. – the Capt. with unremitting attention, standing over them all the while, and compelling them to make all clean. – He is still as partial to me, as ever he was, and will do any thing to promote the comfort of my family. – And were it not for the heat, we would be pretty comfortable. Lat: 12:5 – Ther: 80 in the shade. – Knots 5, or 6. –

21st. Tuesday. – A fine morning; but very warm: – Catharine ill with headach, owing to the heat. – light breeze about noon. – our twilight very short, both in the morning and evening – rays of the sun uncommon bright, and warm. – Lat: 10.39. rate about 3 miles an hour. Therm: 82. to bed about 11. by far the most sultry night we have hitherto had; the Ther: 82, at 10 at night. –

22. – Wednesday. – obliged to go upon deck, about ½ past 1 this morning, owing to the great heat below. – find many sleeping on deck, under coverings. – got very little rest this night. – towards day light had a light breeze which continues through the day. – we are now getting out of the N.E. trade-winds, and expect the breeze to be very changeable, until we cross the line and reach the S.E. Trades. – The Sun now the N. of us. – the appearance of the constellations much altered, and many new ones coming into view, and the N.pole very low. – the Sickness is decreasing, and we are beginning to be seasoned with the heat. – we make very little use of our Coats, vests, and neck-Clothes; at least we never take them to Table with us; and still we perspire freely. – Lat: 9:36. Ther. 83. –

23rd. Thursday. A fine; but sultry morning. – after breakfast went upon deck, and observed the appearance of a Thunderplump. – this was about ½ past 9, and in course of 10 minutes, it became very dark. – The greater part of the sails being hauled down; we were all ordered to go below. – in a little time, a strong gale, tremendous rain: but little thunder. – and now we had a keen scramble, who to catch most fresh water. – I got about 3 gallons, and we found it very refreshing, although, (not having had any

The Port of Leith, 1824, by Alexander Nasmyth. The *Symmetry* left from here for the Argentine in May, 1825. *City Art Centre, Edinburgh.*

The Port of Buenos Aires, 1834, by Richard Adams. The *Symmetry* arrived off Buenos Aires in August, 1825. *Museo Nacional de Bellas Artes, Buenos Aires.*

Coming ashore by bullock cart.

The main Plaza of Buenos Aires.

Gaucho with lasso.

The Haycutter.

General Rosas.

Two of Rosas' soldiers.

Interior of a *pulpería*.

Transport in the interior.

Gauchos, photographed later in the century, feet on horned skulls.

Rev. William Brown.   Rev. James Smith.

St. Andrew's 'Rancho' Kirk, Chascomús. The illustrations on this page are
reproduced from James Dodds, *Records of the Scottish Settlers on the River Plate
and their Churches* (1897), by permission of the Trustees of the National
Library of Scotland.

rain for a long time, and it was Catched from the sails and ropes,) it had a very tarry flavour, – about 1 p.m. a dead sultry calm. – at 6 in the evening more clear, than for sometimes past. – this was a very disagreeable day. Lat: 8:37 – Ther: 82. –

24th. Friday. – calm, sultry morning, so early as 8 o'Clock, the Ther: 80 in the shade. observe a number of Sharks; several speared; but not one taken. – at 10 a.m. appearance of a Shower; in half an hour's time, a brisk gale with rain, and we get on finely. – we are now steering S. by E. to catch the S.E. Trades – a fine afternoon. – we made little of it last night. – Lat: 7.56. Ther: 81 in shade.

25th – Saturday. – A soft morning, and slight rain. a number of sharks following us. – about 10 a.m. one of them took a bait-hook, fastened to a chain and strong rope; and then we had a fine hurry, to see him hauled aboard, and to get out of the way when he reached the deck. – we actually thought that he would have split the deck, as every smack that he gave it, with his tail, made a report like the crack of a pistol. – he was about 6 feet long – the Sailors got a couple of hatchets, and soon despatched him, by cutting off his head, and tail. – he is very powerful; before one stroke of his tail, a man's leg, or thigh, would snap like a straw. – when cut up, bits of bacon, and other refuse, thrown overboard, were found in his maw. – From noon until about 5 in the evening rain fell as if from a water spout: and we got several barrels of it, which answered a good purpose, that of washing. – this was another unpleasant day – Lat: 6.56. Ther: 78.

26th Sabbath. – A fine calm, clear morning, – ½ past 8 the Ther: 83 in the shade: it had the appearance of a storm – we were just sitting down to Breakfast, all things ready. – But our ever vigilant Capt. was at his post: and '*Down Top Royals, Clear Decks*', was the word. – In less than 5 minutes the Hurricane struck us: the sea met us like a mountain: our Tables were upset, and all their furniture went to shivers: every thing at liberty danced like a top; and we were almost heaped upon one another: The rain fell in clouds: we had not much thunder: but the Ladies got awful fright. – The storm was soon over. – the breeze continued right ahead till about noon; it then became fair; but scant. – we had no sermon on deck, all things being in confusion, and much of the rigging to repair. – we got prayers in the Cabin at night. – very warm afternoon. – we weary much for the Trades. – the Capt. to encourage us says 'we must have them soon'. – we have Calm upon Calm. – Lat: 5.53. Ther: from 82 to 83 in the shade. –

27th Monday. – Calm morning, after a dead Calm night, made only 10 miles last 24 hours, the lowest rate since we left Leith. – about 1 p.m. a fine breeze. – all well to day. – Lat: 5.43. Ther: 81. rate towards evening 4 Knots: going on fine. –

28th Tuesday. – A fine morning, any little wind that we have is right ahead. – Tacking. – small progress. – about 1 p.m. a breeze right ahead. – considerable swell. – Lat: 5.15. Ther: 79. – getting cooler. –

29th Wednesday. – Fine morning. – steady breeze right ahead – about 2 p.m. wind more favourable. – Capt. thinks we approach the Trades. – very warm in the sun. – not so sultry. – Lat: 4.25. Ther: 80. –

30th Thursday. – A calm, clear, warm morning – pleasant, but rather warm day. – wind pretty fair; but scant. – Lat: 3.20. – This day's Longitude 20.51 W and the Ther: 81. –

JULY, 1825

1st. Friday. – A fine morning. – no progress. – we have gained the Trades. – they are too much from the South, being right ahead. – we are perfectly weary of this slow kind of work. – Lat. 2.31 N. Ther: from 78 to 80 in the shade. –

2nd. Saturday. – Fine morning. – Course S.W. near the wind. – Tack to the E. – we would have crossed the Line a week ago, had we not been between the Trades. we have wearied more the last fortnight, than we did during the whole of the Voyage. – We are told it is fine weather to be so near the Line. – we have heard very little Thunder. – none any way near us. – Lat: 1.8N Ther: 80. – it has been a fine day; and is a pleasant Evening. –

3rd. Sabbath. – A fine morning. – steady breeze from the S. – Cross the Line at 9 a.m. – Public worship on deck at ½ 10. – a good turnout. – our water very bad. – can use none of it, till after it has been boiled, – our allowance of porter, ½ a bottle a man, daily; we could never do without it. – the Ceremony, observed upon passing the Line, delayed till tomorrow. – hitherto our Latitude has been N. – henceforward, if we be not driven back, it will be S. – and the North pole is set, to rise no more. – we are now entering a new world. – our Latitude is always calculated at noon; to day we were Lat: 0.10, or 10 miles south of the Line. – or in sea phrase 10 Knots S. – Ther: 78. – getting cooler.–

4th Monday: A fine morning. – The Sailors claim use and wont, upon crossing the Line. – the Capt. will not allow any thing to be done to any of the Passengers. – we promise them Grog. – this was just what they wanted. – in the evening there was fine diversion between the old and young Sailors. – it ended all in fun, and a few of them tipsy. – wind veering towards the E. – Lat. 2:S. Ther. 79. –

5th Tuesday. – A fine morning. – fair wind; getting on fine. – greater flocks of flying fish. – they seem stronger than any we had seen before, as they rose pretty high. – about the size of herrings. – this is a fine day all well. – Lat: 3.55. Long: 26.32. Ther: 78. rate 5 Knots – now opposite Brasil coast. –

6th Wednesday – An excellent morning – steady, fair breeze. – we are now in the S.E. Trades. – and we expect they will continue till we reach the Plata. all in good health, and high spirits, going on so finely. – Lat. 6.17 – Ther: 78 – rather sultry Rate 6 Knots. – we have not made so fine a day's sailing, for some time back.

7th Thursday.– Nothing new: all things agreeable. – The Sultry region, of which, it is hoped, we are taking farewell, rather spoiled our sports, which we are now reassuming: a game at draughts, or Backgammon: sometimes a rubber at whist, in the evening. – The Capt. and I oft on a side. – no gambling allowed – all for amusement; whatever the game may be. – it now gets dark about ½ past 6 – and we generally go to bed about 11. – Lat: 8.28 – Ther: 78. rate of 6 Knots. – all well: going on fine. –

8th Friday. – Everything according to our wish. – The Dr. was called from Breakfast; and in the course of 15 minutes, when we reached the deck, word was sent up that we had got another passenger. – The wife of one of Mr. Broache's Ploughmen was safely delivered of a fine girl, – mother and child doing well. – we were now 213 strong. – no shipping in view. – Lat: 10.40. Ther: 78. rate from 7, to 9 Knots. –

9th Saturday – All Things favourable going on finely. – A Committee appointed to report to Mr. Robertson, as to the state of our provisions: I proposed Mr. McClement, and Mr. Galbrath; but I was outvoted, and the rest being unanimous, Mr. Fisher, and Mr. Johns were elected. – we are now all in high spirits, and longing for a sight of the promised land. – we had two Pigs killed today; as we have always a good dinner on Sabbath, which is tomorrow. – I never lived better, all my life. – we have fresh-pig, fine preserved soup, which was prepared in London, and which we relish much: plenty of rice pudding, and fine flour for bread: – our beef, and water, only, are disagreeable: and even the water, after being boiled, and cooled is not so bad as one might expect. – Lat: 13.18. Lon: 31.36. – Ther: 78. –

10th Sabbath. – A fine morning: breeze rather lighter; but quite steady from the E. – Public worship on Deck. – it was well attended. – this is delightful weather. – we do not feel it disagreeably warm. – perhaps from having lately left the sultry tracts of the Line. – The days are creeping in. – the sun sets before 6. – no appearance of any shipping. – I have had a letter prepared, for some time past, for Miss Montgomerie: but no opportunity of forwarding it. – This evening the Capt. and I retired, by ourselves, and read 3, or 4 Sermons. – Lat: 15.55 – Lon: 32.44. – Ther: 78, to 79. – and rate from 6½, to 4½ Knots. –

11th Monday. – Fine morning – breeze light, from the S. – carrying us too much to the W. – unless when calm, not too warm. – at 3 p.m. a sail in view – bring up my letter to Miss M. – They passed us to leeward – it blew pretty hard at the time – could not speak them – distant about two leagues. – we and they both hoisted English colours. – Capt. thinks they are homeward bound. – Lat: 17.7 – Lon: 34.2 Ther: 75. – rate 4 Knots.

12th Tuesday. – a fine morning, and steady breeze. – observe a number of Whales, spouting in different places; but too distant for a perfect view. – they throw the water pretty high. – a fine day Lat: 18:56. – Ther: 74, always in the shade. – rate 7 Knots. –

13th Wednesday. – A fine morning, breeze scanty. – making little way. – about 11 a.m. observe more whales; three of them came along side. – the nearest might be 60 yards distant. – got a full view of it. – it has a Greenish appearance. – while it blew, the greater part of its back was above water, and we could observe a very long fin. – They swim very quick. – we are making little progress. – Lat. 20.24 – Lon: 36.28. – very warm Ther: from 76 to 79. –

14th Thursday. – A calm, warm morning. – about noon a breeze strikes up. – at 2 p.m. an appearance of a thunder storm. – at 3 a little rain, no thunder. – a fine evening. – at 8 the lightning began to flash. – at 10, it appeared towards S.W. one continued blaze, much like what we have observed the aurora-borealis in Scotland, – the Mate says it indicates a storm. – it kept at a distance. – to bed ½ 10. Lat: 21.49. – Lon: 38. Ther: 78. rate in afternoon 6½ Knots. –

15th. Friday. – Awaked, about ½ past 12 midnight, by an unusual noise. – all was hurry upon deck, nothing but trampling and shouting. – in a minute the Hurricane came upon us like a whirl-wind. – The shock made us all turn out of bed, in an instant. – the ship trembled; the Capt. called, the sailors roared; the sails clashed; the ropes cracked. the Ladies screamed; the crockery clattered; the children cried. – surprise seized me, and I cannot tell what I felt. – I ran to the cabin door and peeped out. – most awful!! the extremes of light and darkness succeeded each other instantaneously; one second you could distinguish the most minute object, the next you could see nothing; the rain fell like a torrent. – we had no thunder; but the lightning was very vivid. – It was one of those confusions of nature, which the sailors term a Pamperies, frequent in those climes; and of which nothing but experience can communicate any adequate conception. – we seemed to be in its very centre, at the dead hour of a very dark night, for it was near new moon, and roused from a sound sleep. – it came in an instant, and continued about the space of 20 minutes. – and then we had a dead calm. – The swell continued sometime longer. – I went upon deck so soon as it began to subside: the Capt. told me the worst was over. – every sail was down; the sea rolled terribly; and in the morning the deck was covered with sand: whence it had come nobody could tell, only it has been frequently observed to be the case. – we got under sail about 2, and I returned to bed about ½ an hour thereafter. – I believe none of us passengers had ever, at any former period, got such a surprise: and had sufficient cause to confess 'that we were frightened'. about 9 a.m. a fine morning; but showery looking: we had been carried a considerable way to the E. by the squall, as we had been sailing yesterday's afternoon, and last night towards the W. wishing to get near the land, expecting the wind from it. – Lat: 23.2 – Lon: 38.3. Ther: 75 – rate at 4 p.m. about 8 Knots an hour:

16th Saturday. – We had a squall this morning about 1 o'clock, with a shift of wind to the W. reached the deck about 7. – fine breeze, right ahead, with a heavy swell. – making little way. – as sail right ahead schooner rigged: she crosses us to windward: the Capt. thinks 'she may be a slaver for the Coast of Africa'; cannot speak her. – made little to the S. a good way to the W. – not far from the Brasil Coast, opposite rio-Janeiro; near the Tropic of Capricorn. – a number of sea fowls pay us a visit – hook several of them; one of a pretty large kind, being 6 feet between the tips of the wings when extended. – there were four different kinds of them – some of very beautiful plumage, would have been pretty, had they been stuffed; but none of us Knew any thing of the art: – Lat: 23.33 – Lon: 41. now getting cool. – Ther: 71 in the shade. – rate southward very slow.

17th Sabbath. – Mount deck about 7. wind more favourable being S. by E. – observe a sail far to the windward, whether a schooner or a Brig could not say. – public worship on deck; well attended. – a couple of roasted pigs at Dinner, much relished. – our water bad; alas! what is much worse, our Porter done!! – working away with our boiled water. – this was a very pleasant settled-looking day. – fine and cool. – Lat: 24.28. – Lon. 43. Ther: 68. – rate 5 ks. –

18th Monday. – reach deck ½ past 6. – a delightful morning. – all in high spirits, as we are going on fine. – a Cask of Porter discovered in the hold, which had been lost: this is joyful news. – for our water is undrinkable; when we can get Porter. – a most beautiful evening. – The Magic Clouds[23] make their appearance – two small white ones, towards the E. and a large black one in the South. – the Sailors tell us these are the Clouds, which attended the Israelites in the Desert. – be that as it may; they affirm that they are always seen in the same place. – the constellations are most brilliant. – Lat: 26.14. Lon: 43.33, – rate 6 Knots. Ther: 68. –

19th Tuesday. – Wind right N. all in the highest spirits. – blowing strong and steadily. – the sea very Rough. – never knew what sailing was till to day – the highest rate since we left Leith being 9 Knots. – to day as below. – Lat: 28.33, Lon: 44.54. rate from 7, to 12½ Knots. Ther: 70. –

20th Wednesday. – A squally morning, wind fair, after a capital night. – all life, soul, and mirth. going on so finely. – at 9 a.m., a shower. – at 10, almost Calm. – wind more to the west. – at 11 the Breeze springs up. – Since yesterday at noon until to day, at noon, we had run 249 miles, being 10 ½ miles at an average, for the last 24 hours. – at 7 in the evening all on Deck, being a calm beautiful night. – Fiddle, Flute, and Bagpipe struck up all at once, and our Swains,[24] and

23. This is a reference to the cloud which guided the Israelites from place to place in the Desert of Sinai after the establishment of the Dwelling/Tabernacle: 'Now at the time that the Dwelling was set up, the cloud covered the Dwelling over the Tent of Testimony, and after sunset it remained over the Dwelling, as the appearance of fire, until daybreak . . . According as the cloud was lifted up from the tent, after that the Children of Israel would march on, and in the place that the cloud would take-up-dwelling, there the Children of Israel would encamp . . . Whether two days or a New-Moon or a year-of-days, when the cloud lingered over the Dwelling, dwelling over it, the Children of Israel would remain-in-camp, and would not march on; at its lifting-up, they would march on' (Numbers 9: 15-22). This quotation is taken from *The Five Books of Moses: A New Translation with Introductions, Commentary, and Notes by Everett Fox* (London: The Harvill Press, 1995).

24. *Swain*: an archaic term meaning 'a country youth', or, in poetic usage, 'a young lover or suitor' (*Oxford English Reference Dictionary*).

Nymphs made the deck rebound, and showed that 8000 miles of Sea had not cooled their Scottish blood, nor all the Sultry force of the Torrid Zone sunk their Physical powers, while they Danced the Highland-fling, with all its honours, mirth and glee: no doubt, to the amazement of the watery Elfs of these climes, who never saw the like before: but for my own part I fancied myself in the land of cakes, celebrating some Harvest-home, or Scottish Nuptials. – It had a fine effect upon all, young and old. – when retired to the Cabin, we dedicated an hour or two, to some of Burns' most Patriotic lays, and 'Mirth went round and cheerful chat.' – We heaved dull Care overboard, and retired to bed praying for another such Gale to waft us up the Plata, being all satisfied of Sailing. – Lat: 31.8. – Lon. 48.7 – rate variable, in the morning as high as 10 Knots, but declines with the calm towards night. Ther: 70 in the shade. –

21st Thursday. – A dull looking morning: – gained little way, and doing little. – turns out the most pleasant day that I ever saw. – the Capt. says it is uncommon at this Season. – Lat: 32.12. Lon: 49. Ther: 69. rate 5 Knots: but often very low, having many calms. – The Sun sets to night exactly 10 minutes past 5. –

22nd Friday. Very early up. – dull and stormy-like. – the wind shifts right ahead and puts us upon a tack: in a little bit it becomes more favourable, being S. by E. still we are getting firmly on, though the sea is a little roughish. – we hope to see Cape St. Mary[25] tomorrow. – Lat: 33.31. Lon: 50.16. Ther: 60. being rather a cold day. – rate about 5, or 6 Knots. –

23rd Saturday. – About 4 in the morning, awakened by the sailors taking down the Sails, preparatory to another Pamperies: got up and peeped out; the lightning was most vivid; more so than on the former occasion, and the Storm seemed at hand. – the squall came after about half an hour, with some rain, which did not continue long; the blast came right ahead and carried us Eastward. – the rain was soon over; but the gale increased to a hurricane, sweeping all before it. – I went upon deck about 6. it was blowing hard; little rain, no thunder: – The Capt. feared it was not at the worst, and that it would continue for some time. – They lightened the

25. *Cape St. Mary* (or Cabo Santa María): a promontory near the small port and resort town of La Paloma, Department of Rocha, Uruguay.

rigging as much as possible and by 4 p.m. Top, and Top-royal masts were taken down, and not a yard was left – and still the gale seemed only beginning. – we were all ordered to bed at an early hour of the night: the sea was very rough: – we were ill disposed for sleep, and very unhappy. – the vessel pitched much: but very little water came upon deck. it was an awful night. – Much worse than the Bay of Biscay. – Lat: 34.21. Lon: 52.31. Ther: below deck 54. a cold day, when we went out we had to put on our great coats, having hailshowers, rate pretty quick; but rather Back as forward.

24th Sabbath. – Early on deck, having slept little during the night. – The sea rose into hills, and the spray rose like sleet; nothing but foam, as far as the eye could reach: nothing of the appearance of water remained. – The deep seemed transformed into hillocks covered with Snow, drifting from one to another. – every thing of rigging kind, was taken down to case the Masts, now bending under their own weight. – only one little sail, having four reefs in it was left standing, without which we could not lie to; and thus we lay to wind. – between 3 and 4 p.m. a ship under bare poles, drifting before the wind passed close to our stern. – we hoisted English Colours, and they those of Brasil. – our mate spoke her – she was from Brasil bound for the Plata. – They did not show any Longitude. – our Capt. thought they had lost themselves as they ran right from the river. – He held up a board with our Lon: marked upon it, to them, and when we were about a mile past them, they turned and lay to the wind. – and so we remained during the night. – Lat: 34.40. Lon: 52.10 Ther: 53 below deck, cold, rain, and sleet, with hail. – rate lying to Wind. –

25th Monday. – A rough morning. reach the Deck about break of day. – we think the worst is over, and make a tack: but can do little. – a sail in view, far distant; the one mentioned yesterday. – The wind slackens toward evening, and becomes more favourable. – Lat: 34.43 – Lon: 51.30. Ther: 55 in shade rate very low, as to the right way. –

26th Tuesday. – A strong, side breeze, a sail in view, but distant; on a different course: – about 4 p.m. wind more favourable; getting on finely. – at 6, a strong breeze, and much lightning: about 10, it came upon us in perfect streams, very vivid, and quite terrific. – the Ladies were much alarmed: – Our Mate said 'he had been often in these latitudes: but never saw the Lightning so bright'. – we had a shower of rain, with a little thunder, and then a calm: we had drifted about 150 miles Eastward, during the storm. Lat: 34.41. Lon: 49.4. – Ther: 58. – a cold day: rate at one time, to day, about 9 Knots. but variable.

27th Wednesday. – A fine morning, almost calm. – gaining little. – nearing the land. as we observed a quantity of sea- weed floating about. this was a fine calm day, with now and then a breeze. – We got rather too far S. to day. – Lat: 35.10: Lon: 52 rate 5 K. but very unsteady.

28th Thursday. A most beautiful morning, after a good deal of thunder: Soundings last night about 12 o'clock, being the first 60 Fathoms: this morning 25 Fath: this was encouraging. – about 25 miles from land, which we expect to see tomorrow-morning. – this was a fine day; but cold. – Lat: 34.38. – Lon: 53.25. – Ther: 52. – Soundings, at noon 25 Fath: wind ahead: tacking when we go to bed. –

29th. Friday. – 'LAND! LAND! *LAND* in View!!!' – The Spirit-moving sound of the watch, about daybreak, wakens us all. – all spring out of bed, rush upon deck, and behold, the long sought, much wished for Land. – it was Land: it was Cape St. Mary. – it appeared at a distance – we had passed it in the night – our first view was faint. not yet being fully light – we were sailing along the shore. with the wind from the S. – a fine morning after a squally night. about noon we neared the shore and got a full view of the Land. we were about 3 miles from it, in 14 Fathoms water. – the shore has a rocky appearance, and the water seemed to be beating much upon it as we observed the spray to rise pretty high. – The Land seemed level, bleak, and gently rising as it proceeded from the Shore. – we observed a few houses: they appeared to be flat roofed: but our view at this time was indistinct; as we were forced to tack, the wind blowing right from the river. – this was a cold day, and we had on our great Coats. – making little way; the Current was pretty strong, the wind ahead; and we were struggling against wind and water. Ther: 44 upon deck, and 50, below. –

30th Saturday, a sharp, cold, dry morning: but alas!! we are farther to the E. than we were yesterday at the same time of day, and all that we had gained by day we have lost in the night. – !!! Winds of Columbia[26] beat us not from your shore. – We are the Sons of Liberty. – we come to you because you are free. – we come to hail your Emancipation. – we bring you not fetters, slavery, nor Inquisition. – our prowess lies in the muscles of our arms, our weapons are the Implements of Ceres;[27] her Seeds are in our Hold; our weather-beaten hands shall adorn your plains; we will become your Sons; our blood will mingle with yours, and Columbian, and Briton shall have no distinction. – for, indeed, we are all weary of cross winds, and flashing storms. –

31st. Sabbath. A fine dry, cold morning. – wind fair, and we are getting on finely. – Land in view; the Isle of Lobos, or Seal Island. – it appears nothing but rocks. – we passed pretty nigh it – it lies right in the mouth of the river, and is frequented for seals and seafowl. – we are now 60 miles from Mount Video. – where we expect to Anchor during night. – We expected by this time to have been in fresh water; but still it is pretty salt: but nothing like the sea. – a sail right ahead, going up the river. – about 11 a.m. we come along side, and hail her, whence and whither, 'from Brasil, bound to Mount Video', was the answer. – She hailed us in turn; we answered, 'from Britain, bound to Buenos Ayres'. – we passed her in grand style – she was only a little brig, and we soon left her far behind: the Crew seemed mostly Spaniards: only the man who spoke us, our Capt. affirmed to be an Englishman, as he spoke the English language quite naturally. they wore, mostly, red Caps, and had a very sallow complexion. – about 3, we came in view of M. Video. – ½ past 3 we pass the Isle of Flores,[28] and at 4, we are opposite M.V. – within about 4 miles of it. – The town lies low, at the bottom of a round, high hill. – there appears to be a fort, or castle on the side of the town next to the shore, with three towers upon it, which, when at a distance, appeared to be ships. – we understood there had been a light house upon the hill, but, as our Capt. thought it unsafe to proceed during night through we lay to, yet light made its appearance. This was a fine day; but cold Ther: 48. –

26. *Columbia*: a poetic synonym for the Americas.
27. *Ceres*: the Roman goddess of corn.
28. *Isle of Flores* (or Isla de Flores): a small rocky island in the River Plate, a short distance south-east of Montevideo, the site of a lighthouse.

AUGUST, 1825

1st. Monday. – I reached the deck about daybreak: we were under full sail, and had to cross the river, to the south side where we were to turn up to Buenos Ayres: – a Pilot came alongside: – he asked 120 Dollars to take us up to the roads: – our Capt. thought it much; but he (the P.) would take no less, and so left us. – We were now in sight of Land on the Buenos Ayres side, and had not gone far from the place, where the Pilot left us, when the ship gave a *thump* upon the bottom, and '*down Sails, Ship about*' were the orders; these were done with despatch. (the vessel striking and beating freely upon the sand all the while), and we very soon got into deeper water, when all was right again. – All the passengers were upon deck, at the time. – we were all much surprised, the Captain himself seemed highly alarmed, not expecting anything of the kind, and the Ladies were screaming in every direction, and frightened, almost to distraction. this was the worst of all, that we had yet met with: and, *indeed*, our first salutes from Columbia (for this was the first touch) were stamped upon our minds with indelible impressions. – Catharine seems much agitated, and I feel the more on her account. – about 4 p.m. being on the mid-channel way, we came in view of two masts, which, upon inspection, with the Glass, our Capt. found to be a Brig, sticking fast upon a Sand bank, on the very course that he intended, and eminent as he was, here he appeared to be nonplussed. – as this case required caution, he ordered 'Ship-about', and dropped Anchor, for the night, (intending to attempt the inland passage in the Morning,) with 3 ½ Fathoms water. – He (the Capt.) then observed to me, that he would give £50, for a Pilot, as the bed of the river was altered very lately, or his Chart was wrong laid down. – This had been a disagreeable day to us all, in various respects: but we now expect a sound night's sleep: as this is the first time that our Anchor has been down, since we left the Forth; exactly 10 weeks and one day ago; being on Sabbath May the 22 ult. –

2d. Tuesday. – mount deck at daylight. – all anxious to get up the river. we hoist sail. and the wind being fair, we proceed about 7 miles an hour with a regular depth of water, being about 4 Fathoms, and all upon the

outlook for what is called the Chaco sand Bank. – after a little time a
Buoy was descried. and so soon as our Capt. had got its colour, by the
Glass: '*all well, more sail*' was the word: more Sail is hoisted, and we go on,
all well. – after we had got clear of the shoals, 3 sail right ahead meeting us:
the one next us backed sails and lay to. – all 4 of us had up English
Colours. – we hoisted first. and they, all 3, soon did the same. – our Capt.
knew the one lying to, at first sight, caused the boat to be lowered, and
sent the Mate aboard. – after a little the Boat returned, and took the Capt.
aboard. – I had an old letter, which I had written to Miss Montgomerie,
when we were about the Cape Verds: – I inserted in the inside of it the
day of the Month, and where we were, and sent it aboard. – They passed
very near us, and were, the Resignation of Scarborough, the Waterloo of
London, and the Hope of Liverpool, all bound for Liverpool. – we gave
them 3 Cheers, as they came along side, which they returned. – we were
now in sight of the Roads, the end of our Voyage – we moved gently on:
the evening was calm, and foggy – we dropped Anchor in Buenos Ayres
Roads about 7 in the evening, and so ended our voyage, as we had begun
it under darkness, and amidst fog, after a passage of 72 ½ natural days, or
73 days and 72 nights, reckoning by light and darkness, or artificially.
Catharine not well to day, I impute her sickness to be the consequence of
yesterday's surprise, when we struck the bank. – we retire to bed about
11, hoping for a sound sleep, and expecting a view of the Country, and
City tomorrow-morning. –

3rd. Wednesday. Early up, after a good night's sleep. – Nothing but fog
to be seen. – in a little it clears somewhat, so that we can observe the
Shipping. – after Breakfast the Capt. and Dr. go ashore, with their reports,
the one for the Customs, the other for the state of our health. – when in
the Boat we give them 3 hearty cheers. – they do not return till late. – we
were anxious to hear the news – this day very wet and foggy – and their
report to us not very flattering. the Capt. promises to take me along with
him tomorrow, that I may judge from sight. – a very disagreeable day. –

4th Thursday. – Early up; a fine morning. – The Capt. and 5 of us go
ashore. – the first thing that attracts our attention are the Horses. – Pretty
little, well trained animals. – surely very excellent horsemen. – the
Bullocks are handsome and fine drawers. – Their Carts very clumsy,

the wheels about 7 feet high. – the Streets a complete puddle: unpaved, excepting as much as will allow two people to walk abreast, along the front of the houses. – the Houses low, flat roofed, and very dark looking. – Call at Mr. Robertson's Counting-room. – he is not in. – Speak, and dine with his head Clerk: meet, there, with a Mr. Park, a Scotchman, whom Mr. R. had engaged to put in crop upon the property, whither we are going. – he (Mr. P.) gives us a very flattering report of the Country. – They accompany us to the river-side, and we return aboard. – before we parted with Mr. P. it was agreed that we should attend upon him early next morning: he was to prepare horses, and we were to take a ride, and see the lands, and consult about accommodations for our families. – he says it is about 14 miles distant. – a fine day. –

5th Friday. – A very blowy morning. – The wind right from the land. – 6 of us get into the boat, to go ashore. – forced to return after toiling 2 hours, not being able to reach the shore, though we were strongly manned. – write two letters to Scotland, one to My Father, and the other to Miss Montgomerie: to be sent by the Packet, which sails tomorrow at noon. – this was a cold, stormy day. – we had plenty of fresh provisions sent us, last night, by Mr. Robertson's orders. –

6. Saturday. Blowing pretty hard. – wind more favourable. – after Breakfast, the Capt. and a few get into the Boat about ½ past 8: but do not reach the shore till about 12. – did not go out to day, on account of Catharine's indisposition. – part of those who went were to go into the Country, to view the place of our destination. – in the evening the Capt., Dr. and a few who had been with them returned, and brought us flattering reports about agriculture: but we paid little attention to their second hand stories, as we expect our own spies to return, tomorrow. – they were to take a general look, and to be as correct as possible. – This has been a very cold day. –

7th Sabbath. – This is a fine morning. – Our Spies return about 4 p.m. Mr. Park, and Mr. Robertson's head Clerk, being along with them. – They have a very favourable opinion of the Land: but the houses are very bad. – They say there is one very good house, which may accommodate three of our families, until better be provided. – These reports revive our drooping spirits, and we hope to do well. – Mr. P. and the Clerk, after drinking Tea, with us, return ashore. – This has been a fine day. –

8th Monday. – A pleasant morning. – after Breakfast went ashore with the Capt. and Dr. – call at Mr. Robertson's Office; when there, meet with a Mr. Barton from Scotland: I had a letter to his Lady and a Gold ring, from her friends in Edinr. – I found him a very intelligent man and disposed to give me all the information in his power, he told me that the Land, whereto we were going, once belonged to him: but that he had sold it to Mr. R. not long ago: that he lived some time in the Country, and that he had built a house in it. – he spoke favourably of agriculture: invited me strongly to his house, and to be sure and bring Mrs. G. alongst with me. – in short he was very free, and offered his services where-ever I thought that he could be of any service to me. – I also met with Dr. Mair, from Scotland, for whom I had two letters. – But, however free we may make with our own Countrymen, or however politely we may be treated by them, I think, that a general acquaintance should be formed with much caution; for I do not look upon the common appearance of the people, here, any way calculated to make the most favourable preposses-sions; and any accounts that we hear of their manners, and conduct, do not belie their aspect. – Every stranger, upon his arrival here, I am told adopts the precaution of carrying fire arms, and, whenever I have been on shore, I had always the Pistols, (which I luckily bot. before I left Edinr.) loaded, in my pocket. – The Capt. and I returned aboard in the afternoon: and we had a visit from the officers of the British Frigate: They drank Tea, and spent the evening with us: They expect to remain in this Station for some time. – Their first Lieutenant is a very pleasant, nice, young Scotsman. – got a pressing invitation to go aboard of them, the first fine day, and to take any of my acquaintances with me, as I thought proper. – a fine day . . .

9th – Tuesday. Blowing very hard, all the morning, we are now very anxious to disembark, and we expected the Lighter here today: but it will be impossible for her to come out. – no it is now a blowy evening. – no Lighter. – we have spent the whole day aboard. – and nothing worthy of being mentioned. –

10th Wednesday – This morning still blows harder than what yesterday did. – we are now very impatient, looking long for the Lighters; but no, they will not dare venture out, and if they were here, we could do nothing, while this gale continues. – now it is night; nothing done, nothing new; on board all day, and no communication with any body . . . a blowy evening, after a violent day of wind attended sometimes with rain. –

11th Thursday. A fine morning, and the appearance of a fine day. – A sail coming up the river; we all wonder what she may be. – as she approaches, we observe the British flag flying; and she turns out to be the *Europe* of Liverpool; sailed thence on the 6th of May, having been more than three months on her passage. – But with this, I must stop, and close this Journal. The day seems fine: the Lighters will be here: we have to disload: expect to be all ashore tomorrow, and to repair to the place of our final destination, in the Country, as soon as possible: Under these circum-stances I find it impossible to continue this, (Journal), any longer. – I kept two (Journals) all the passage, one for my own use, and this for the satisfaction of my friends in Scotland, and which I now forward to them, conformably, to a promise, which I made to some of them before my departure, and to a desire which they then expressed. – I regret that it is not so perfect as I could have wished it: but some of my friends are very good readers, and can easily add or subtract a letter, or even overlook a Grammatical slip, or mend a solecism. We were always in motion, and sometimes things more valuable than word fell wrong among our hands; nay I even sometimes thought when we were tossed up and down, 'that our very minds, and conceptions became unsteady'. – But on this point I will say no more, lest my friends should suspect that I doubt their affection.

Our passage was, what may be termed 'a pretty fair one': we had an excellent sea-boat; she was well manned, and I have elsewhere given my opinion of our worthy Capt. – After we got fairly to sea, unless when a blast came our way, we had less confusion, and sickness than I expected. – The only thing that happened us that can be called unlucky, was our striking the Sandbank: though it actually did us no damage, it had a wonderful effect, and only those, who have been in a similar situation, can conceive the sensation produced by the slight touches, which the ship made upon the sand, and the force it had upon our imaginations. – I regret it not on my own account: but as it made so deep an impression upon Catharine. –

I have observed that the Country seems bleak, the City gloomy, and the aspect of the Inhabitants rather forbidding. – We have certainly seen every thing to disadvantage, and we have carried prejudices alongst with us which we must overcome, before we can form proper, and consistent Ideas. – We left home on the eve of summer; – experienced the Sultry heat, the bright glare, and the debilitating influence of the Torrid Zone, and tropical climes: nay we may say, 'that we have been cast upon these plains from the midst of Thunder and Lightning'. – Yea our Nomenclature must undergo a reform, and the qualities of our Kalendar submit to a very material alteration. – and when we characterise the days, or the Seasons, we must make a complete transfer of qualities, and put summer for winters, Spring for Autumn, long for short, and heat for cold, and so forth. – We must learn that Boreas now blows upon us from the South: that he yet lingers in these plains, that his last embraces are impressive, when he is about to retire to the mountains of Patagonia, or the Cloud surmounting the Andes, where he always sits covered with his snowy Mantle, as he often does upon Benlomond, and Benlawers, in the Land of Cakes. –

I also herewith send a Draught of the Symmetry, as she passed the Madeiras; no bad representation to be done at sea. – it was sketched by Mr. Adams, who went with us as architect.[29] He is from London, a very amiable gentleman, and has a wife and four Children with us. – He and I

29. *Mr. Adams*: Richard Adams, whose architectural skills were employed during the establishment of the Monte Grande colony, went on to become quite a well-known artist in Buenos Aires. One of his works, 'Puerto de Buenos Aires en 1834', an oil-on-canvas view of the scene which greeted travellers to the city as they disembarked, is reproduced on the cover of the present volume. The original is in the collection of the Museo Nacional de Bellas Artes (Buenos Aires), Argentina's principal gallery. Adams's rather two-dimensional representation of the *Symmetry* appears alongside the eighth page of Cecilia Grierson's *Colonia de Monte Grande: Primera y única colonia formada por escoceses en la Argentina* (Buenos Aires: Peuser, 1925). At the time this book was published, the original watercolour sketch was in the possession of the Grierson family, but I have been unable to trace its present whereabouts.

are on the very best terms, and I have a high opinion of him. I intend the Draught as a memento to Catharine Montgomerie Grierson, Waterfoot. – I know that my Friends will regard it, not according to its intrinsic value, but in proportion of my Intention; and that when Catharine Montgomerie Grierson, Waterfoot, and her sister Jessie, look upon it, they will be put in mind 'that it was the ship, which carried us to Buenos Ayres'; when they observe the small dots intended to represent the passengers peeping over the Bulwarks, it will be observed to them 'that we were amongst them', and that we have sent them this ship for the purpose of bringing them, (for this, or some one like it must bring them) to us, at Buenos Ayres.

To conclude, I hope that we are, now, all out of danger, and I cordially unite with my fellow passengers in returning thanks to a Kind Providence, who has guided us hitherto in safety; and we humbly look upon him for protection, and a continuation of his bounty, being convinced that we are still in his presence, though far from home, and in the Land of Strangers: and we firmly believe, 'that in these sentiments our Friends will be unanimous with ourselves', when they peruse these memorials of us.

THE END

FAITH HARD TRIED
The Memoir of Jane Robson

FAITH HARD TRIED

I was a little girl of four years old when I came to South America, and can only very faintly remember the voyage, which to my young mind seemed endless. My father, soon after he arrived, finding that things were not as had been represented to him, decided to strike out for himself and went to Cañuelas.[1] At that time, Rivadavia was President and the country was in a most unsettled state. I remember, when we had settled in our new quarters, Father started by buying a milk cow which promptly returned to its previous owner some distance across the camp.[2] Father got it back, but the same thing happened again and on each occasion he had to buy it over again, or at any rate pay something, such was the dishonesty of those amongst whom we lived.

At this time there was no fencing in the camp, so the animals would stray away for leagues[3] if not watched and would mix with the others belonging to neighbouring owners, so Father had a brand made to represent a Scottish thistle and with this all our animals were branded, the sheep having a triangular piece taken out of the ear. I found my parents had to work very hard as they had very little money, so I determined to do something to help. One of the young women who had come out with us had a little baby, and was obliged to help make their living, and as the baby was too young to be entirely alone, I went each day to mind it, and thus commenced to earn money at the age of five years. One day while minding the baby, an *aire* struck me on the neck (this is a shock of bad air and often causes great damage; it will crack or shatter a mirror, glasses, etc. which are often found smashed from the effects of an *aire*). My neck was very painful and I was ill and unable to look after my little charge for some

1. *Cañuelas*: the district surrounding a small town of the same name, lying to the south-west of the great metropolis of Buenos Aires.
2. *camp*: a term commonly employed by Anglo-Argentines (and Falkland Islanders) to describe open country, particularly that employed for the pasture of cattle or sheep. It is derived from the Spanish *campo*, meaning countryside or field.
3. The league, a non-standardised and hence variant measure, is roughly equivalent to 3-3¼ miles. It is the preferred unit of distance throughout Jane Robson's account.

days, so my sister had to go in my place. She did not like this and complained bitterly. Someone hearing this teasingly suggested she should chop off the baby's head, so she promptly produced a weapon with which to do it.

About this time, my mother had a baby who died when a month old. This became known, as my father had to go some leagues to get a little coffin, and the neighbours (Italian and Spanish) came to the house playing guitars, dancing and singing. Mother became alarmed at the wild noise they made. Taking the little dead baby in her arms, my sister by the hand and I running beside her, we ran out by the back of the house and made for some high thistles in which to hide. We had a dear old faithful dog; he came with us, but kept growling and would try to bark so I had to hold his mouth as we were in terror of our hiding place being discovered. Night came on and still the noise went on. I became very sleepy and my head fell into Mother's lap; I was awakened by feeling my face against the little dead baby's. It was a weird position for us all. It now seemed quiet, so Mother said, 'Come Jean⁴ we will go home now.' Very cautiously we peeped out and seeing and hearing no one we approached our house, but what disorder met our eyes; the wretched people, not finding anyone in the house, vented their displeasure by upsetting the things and worst of all had taken everything and left us not a thing to eat. Poor Mother, I remember her distress, and we children were hungry and frightened.

Father had gone quite early in the morning, and to be able to return home that night, had borrowed a horse. When about two leagues from home he dismounted, the horse immediately galloped off to its own home, leaving Father stranded. Night came on and the only thing to do was to find his way home as best he could, but alas, the thistles, or *cardos*, were high and he lost his way. All night he was wandering about, and when in the morning he arrived, his face and hands were bleeding from the *espinas* [thorns] which were sticking into him. In trying to find his way, he had pushed through the thistles. It was long before Mother could remove them all. Poor Mother had been wild with alarm all night, not knowing what had happened to Father. This was such a wild uncertain life after leaving our peaceful Scottish home.

The terrible storms we had at times were sufficiently alarming to strike

4. *Jean*: Scots form of Jane.

terror to the souls of grown persons, how much more so to little children. One day my sister and I were coming from the kitchen to the dining room, she carrying a kettle of boiling water. She was holding my hand as the wind was so high, and I suppose we felt safer holding hands. Anyway, I turned to close the door when a severe flash of lightning struck me. I fell to the ground and for some hours was quite unconscious; my clothes were burned and it was a narrow escape from death, one of the many I have had in my life. Fortunately, I was not carrying the kettle of boiling water, or worse might have happened to me. My sister was quite uninjured and suffered nothing worse than a great fright. I suppose it was a little time before I quite recovered, but I did, and was none the worse for my shock.

From this time, I remember little for a year or two. My parents must have prospered, as they appeared to possess a great many cows and we were very busy milking and making cheese and butter. We all had to work hard, and then the butter and cheese were taken into town (Chascomús[5]) for sale.

One day my mother and Mr. W.[6] went to town for this purpose, and to bring my eldest sister home from school (the only means of getting from place to place was on horseback). Well, on the return journey they had a most alarming and exciting experience. All went well until within two or three leagues from home. They were cantering along, my mother with my sister on behind her, when suddenly three horrible rough looking men came towards them, threatening and muttering, 'Let us kill them first', evidently intending to rob them. It occurred to my mother that it would be best not to appear at all alarmed, not an easy thing to do for she felt very frightened and with reason too. Mother turned and looked round as though she was expecting some companions, and spoke as if one was coming along. The men evidently thought that probably this one might have money, so they would get what they could from him and then settle with Mother and her companion, for they galloped off. Mother said, 'Now Mr. W., our only chance is to hide in the *cardos*', but

5. *Chascomús*: a small town lying just over 60 miles south of the city of Buenos Aires.
6. Throughout Jane's account, most of the friends and neighbours of her family are identified only by initials, thus preserving their privacy when there is no good reason for disclosure.

he said, 'My horse will never face them.' Mother said, 'Then I will go first.' She was on a very fiery animal, so turning the horse and facing him towards the thistles she gave him some hard cuts with her whip. The horse made a tremendous jump and sprang right into the midst of the thistles. In her excitement, Mother had forgotten my sister, who was seated behind her, and the poor little girl fell off. As the way was somewhat cleared now and Mother's horse had given the lead, Mr. W.'s animal, after some persuasion, followed and they pushed their way a little distance, the horses and riders getting terribly scratched and torn. Very soon they heard the galloping of horses. It was their would-be murderers returning. At this moment, Mother remembered my sister and exclaimed, 'Oh, my God, my child.' Finding her gone she knew she must have fallen where her horse made his big jump, and not hearing her call she imagined she must have been severely hurt or killed. Her feelings were indescribable, that her poor little child was left to the tender mercy of those ruffians. Her first impulse was to rush back, never mind the consequences to herself, when she heard Mr. W. say in a low tone, 'I have the child.' He had picked her up. She was unconscious for a time, as much from fright as the fall, but soon recovered. Well, they remained scarcely breathing for fear they might be found, when they knew their lives would not be worth a moment's purchase. They could hear the men as they galloped past, vowing vengeance, and no doubt having been baulked and deceived into thinking there was someone whom they could have stolen money from, and finding their other prey also gone, they were in a fearful fury and rushed on full speed hoping to overtake them. Mother waited for some time, and then they went on through the *cardos*, picking places as best they could, hoping to find a way out, and knowing they dared not go back into the road or 'track' again. Then the sun set – such wonderfully glorious sunsets we had too; one wonders looking at the beauty of them how mortals can have such hard and evil hearts – and darkness came on. After that it was still more hopeless. My father was at home, and as night came on he became very alarmed at my mother not appearing, knowing what bad characters were wandering about and that Mother had money with her. He kept walking about, I trotting after him. He did not go to rest that night but kept searching and calling. When morning at last dawned, to our unspeakable relief, the lost ones came, but in such a state, their faces and hands were covered in blood and the horses too were bleeding as the *espinas* of the thistles were sticking into them. They, poor things, had an awful night, trying in vain to find a way home. The first thing to be done was to try and remove the thorns, which Father did with the sheep shears by drawing them lightly over the skin – a primitive but effectual way. I often used this means afterwards in removing thorns from the cattle and horses.

My parents now moved to a place called 'San Vicente', some leagues nearer Buenos Aires. Moving from one part to another in those days was very hard and difficult work, and everyone who could was pressed into the service of helping, we children doing our little bit. It was slow progress across the camp, with no roads and every now and again *pantanos* [marshy areas] to cross. The furniture and all our belongings were in bullock carts, and even when we arrived at our destination we probably had our house to build up. I often think now, with all things arranged so easy for moving, how much fuss people make of insignificant troubles.

One holiday there were a number of girls and boys gathered at our house. A fortune-teller called and commenced (I suppose for a fee of some kind) to tell fortunes. There was great fun and laughter going on. Someone discovered I was not there (I was making the butter) and called me and insisted on my joining the party. The man looked at my hand very gravely, but said nothing; he did not say, as he had to the others, what fate he saw predicted; at this they all said, 'What is Jean's fortune? Oh, she has asked you not to tell.' At this I was vexed and said, 'Yes, tell me, I do not mind.' The fortune-teller said, 'Could I open before you the book of life, the first look at it would kill you. You have a very hard life before you, such a life as few have experienced, and you will feel at times that you cannot battle against it, but through all your many and varied trials you will come out successfully in the end.' I often thought of the man's words, as they proved true.

It was a common thing for people to call at our house as they were travelling through the camp; houses were very far apart. There was a gentleman and his clerks who occasionally came and remained the night. I never liked this man, for one thing I thought him too free. I remember I was much disgusted one day when he said, 'No one would think you girls were Scottish with your white heads and black faces.' We all had very fair hair and our faces were very brown, from sunburn and being always in the air. I retorted, 'No one looking at your red nose would mistake it for anything but a brandy nose.' At this remark he was very angry, and the other men who had been listening to our conversation went outside and exploded with laughter, though they had to be careful not to let the big man know that the laugh was at his expense, for though he liked making rude, personal remarks he did not like others to retaliate, but I never deemed it necessary to study his feelings in the matter. I was always quick at replying, and many times both astonished and annoyed people with my sharp remarks.

My father now joined in partnership with a Mr. and Mrs. G., and they carried on a large dairy farm. Father imported some pigs from home, had quite a large business and did very well. Now I began to work very hard, and as I grew and my strength increased so my many duties became more numerous.

At this time the country was more and more unsettled. Rosas was outside, and Lavalle in, Buenos Aires.[7] There were bands of Indians wandering about who were Rosas's men. Lavalle's soldiers were also wandering about, stealing, murdering and causing the greatest alarm. It was well named 'The Reign of Terror'. It became so terrible that all the families who possibly could went into the town for more safety. My father said that Mother must go with us children, but she said, no, if he could not go she would not leave him. So for a time we remained on, always in danger.

Then an alarming thing happened. It was a common thing for the men (those wandering ruffians) to come to the house and insist on searching it, pretending that they were looking for firearms, and would then steal anything they could lay their hands on. The climax came one day when Father and Mr. G. were away. We had an old peon, who had been a sailor and had lost his arm in one of the many fights and brawls with the Portuguese, I think. He was such a good, faithful old fellow, devoted to Mother and us children. He saw a party of men making for our house so he ran to the door and met them. One of the party dismounted, and drawing his sword commenced threatening and striking the peon. Mother rushed forward and the soldier sheathed his sword, but instead drew his gun and levelled it at her. She, in stepping back to avoid him,

7. This is a reference to the civil war of 1828 to 1829 between Juan Manuel de
   Rosas's Federalists and General Juan Lavalle's Unitarians. The conflict ended
   in victory for Rosas. For further details, see Introduction, pp. 3, 10, and 33.

fell. In an instant our good dog 'Stout' jumped over to protect her, and stood growling and showing his teeth. The brute of a soldier slashed at him with his sword, cutting him to the backbone in three places. The dear old dog still stood his ground though the blood was pouring off him and on to my mother. I then helped to drag Mother up. At this moment a Mr. S., hearing the noise, came flying in, and the men turned their attention to him. He tried to keep their attention occupied until a band of Lavalle's soldiers which he had seen coming, could arrive, but the men sitting on their horses outside saw them also, and, knowing that they would be taken prisoner, gave a shout of warning. They were all on their horses in an instant and galloped off as hard as their horses could go. We afterwards found out that one of these men was an old peon of ours, who had been discharged for doing something wrong. In revenge (and also, no doubt, hoping to get something for himself) he had brought this band of ruffians as he knew that there was money and some valuables in the house, which they intended stealing. He would not have stopped at any crime to gain his ends and be revenged.

All this took place in a short time, but the horror of it was great. Mrs. G., who was in bed with her baby of a day or two old, was nearly dead with fright. My sister fainted, and my mother, though not injured was covered with the blood of our good brave dog, who was now lying dead on the floor. How sad we felt as we looked at his poor torn body. Still, we were thankful that nothing worse had happened to us. From our house these men rode off to a neighbour's house, and presently we heard firing. Mother exclaimed, 'Oh, they have gone to Mr. R.'s and only the boys are at home', and so it turned out. One of the lads tried to protect their home and property, and the man, the leader of the gang, shot him down, poor boy. Then they stole everything they could carry and set the house on fire. I shall never forget the screams and terrors of that day; it was awful.

Father now said that Mother must go into town as it was too dangerous to remain, and after the terrible experience of that day she was quite ready to comply with his wishes, but only on the condition that he came as soon as he possibly could. The next thing was to get us into town safely. Here we had a piece of good fortune. A party of 300 soldiers halted close to our house, and an Officer and some men came to get water and help themselves to any milk we had, so Father, finding the Officer was a nice man, told him his difficulty. He at once said he would give him a pass and an escort, which he did. I shall never forget that journey of many leagues. We had only one cart, and that not a very big one. Into it twelve people were packed, for others as well as our family were thankful for any means to get to safety. Oh, the misery of the jolting and not being able to move one's limbs, so closely were we wedged in. There was no room for luggage, scarcely for the most ordinary necessities. We were comparatively safe after we had passed the camp, and at last we arrived in town, but only to find it full. It was with the greatest difficulty that Mother found a room. The next day Mother and I had to go to the river to get water, as it was very dear to buy and there were no horses or oxen to bring it. I was not feeling well. The river was far out so we had a long distance to go, and before we could return to the shore the water was up to my waist. Directly we reached home with our burden I took off my wet clothes and went to bed as by this time I was feeling very ill. Mother, who was not strong at the time as she had a little baby of two weeks old, also took a chill. The Doctor was called in and said I had measles and must not be in the bed with Mother and the baby. As soon as the doctor left, the woman in whose house we were staying said we must leave at once, as she had a family and could not run the risk of having an infectious disease in her room. What was to be done? Mother could not look for rooms, so a kind friend who heard of our distress said he would see what he could do. After hunting for hours, he returned and said he had found a room but feared it was very damp, but we were thankful for any shelter. He carried me, and other kind friends our mattresses, and Mother was also helped. Thus we arrived at our new quarters. Mother was again taken with violent trembling, and although I was feeling very ill we piled all our clothes on her, and my sister and I had to nurse ourselves and the wee baby as best we could. Well, after a time we got better and things seemed a little brighter for us children. Mother worked very hard, even doing washing, ironing, sewing or anything to make a little money.

I must now tell you of something that happened, which shows how Mother returned good for evil. The woman who turned us out of her house was in great trouble as her two children developed smallpox and were very ill. It was a very bad kind and no one would go to help nurse them. My mother, hearing this, went herself, leaving the baby in our care. She would just come for a few hours, do what was necessary for us, and then return to the nursing. The children recovered, and none of us took the disease. Years after my parents did still more for this family. The husband failed in business, and they took them into our house and educated their boy.

Now to return to the time when my father came to join us in town. After we left the camp there was only my father and our old sailor servant. (I mentioned him as having lost an arm. He had been one of White-lock[e]'s men, and often told us many curious tales of those adventurous times.)[8] They had to undergo endless hardships and finally had to flee for their lives. Some soldiers found them and took everything they possessed, even their clothes, and left them tied hand and foot. My father thought they would starve to death, but the old peon cheered him by saying, 'This is not the first time I have been bound, I will get free', and sure enough he did, and loosened my father. Then, they thought, what were they to do, for they were absolutely naked. Their only chance was to get to the camp and throw themselves on their mercy, though they feared there was little chance of sympathy or help from that quarter. It was the only alternative, however, so they went and pleaded for even a few rags. Those they did get, but scarcely enough to cover their nakedness, and in this state Father arrived in town. Now came a time of many privations, and Father did any work he could get, and, as I said before, Mother was working hard also. At last the Revolution came to an end and Rosas was in power.

People began to return to the camp and their homes, and our parents decided to go also. They were feeling sad and anxious, as they did not know if they would find anything left of their home. Alas, there was little indeed left. Everything that would burn had gone, and there was nothing left but ashes.

We now had to start our life afresh, and very up-hill work it was. The first thing to be done was to build our house, working literally day and night until it was accomplished. Then Father hired cows, milked them, and made butter and cheese for sale. Gradually we once more got cattle of our own. As I have said before, we had no means of keeping our animals

8. We thus learn that the servant had taken part in Lieutenant-General John Whitelocke's assault upon Buenos Aires in 1807, which resulted in ignominious defeat for the British forces at the hands of the local population, the same fate they had suffered the previous year after a brief occupation of the city. These events are remembered in Argentine historiography as the *invasiones inglesas* (English invasions).

from straying to other camps except by watching them constantly. Natives had a way of planting corn, and then, if one's cattle went into it, they would charge heavily for damage done. Now I was very strong and the life I was leading made me even more so each week. I was constantly on horseback and was as fearless as the wind. Indeed, I did not know the meaning of fear, nor have I all my life. Whatever the weather, sun or wind, rain or storm, I was out early in the morning and home late at night. I was doing peon's work by looking after the cattle. I remember sometimes, when we would go out in the cold winter mornings, the mud would be hard from frost, but as soon as the sun rose it would melt and we would be up to our knees in cold slush and mud, for we had neither stockings nor boots.

My eldest sister was not strong, so had none of this life, and was sent into town to school. I began to feel that I would also like to be learning, and when Father had half an hour to spare he would give me lessons, but these were very rare occasions. I had evidently a good memory, for I never forgot anything I had learned.

Now came a *seca* [drought] for three years, and times were very hard with us again; there was no grass for the animals, and they became thin and weak and died. This meant ruin once again. A most curious thing happened at this time, it rained mice, at any rate so it was said, for we had a pest of them, and no one knew from where they had come if not from the sky. After a time I had the opportunity of having a few lessons at a house three leagues away, but as some days I could not go as there would be work needing my care and I had to remain at home, it was not very satisfactory, so my lessons had to be given up and for a time things went on as usual. One day I cried to my mother and said, 'Everyone can get some education but me and I shall grow up not knowing anything of books; I work day and night to get some education, but something always stops me.'

Now there was a Mrs. P. who had a school for little girls in her house, so Father said I might go and see what she would charge to take me for a time (I was only 12 years old). I went off, delighted, but Oh dear! my heart was very heavy when she told me her terms; I knew Father could not pay so much. Suddenly I thought Mrs. P. must have a great deal to do herself; so I said to her that if she would let me do the housework and look after the small girls I would work very hard for her and she could give me some lessons in return. She readily agreed to this. I would rise early and work very hard, but I feared I did not do enough and said so one day to Mrs. P. She put her hand on my head and said, 'God bless you, you are a great comfort to me.' I remained with her six months, and I may say that was all the education I ever had. My mother had a fall from her horse, and I was sent for as they could no longer spare me.

Shortly after this Father bought a piece of ground and built on it. He called it New Caledonia. It was close to the *chacras* [fields], and when we had a windy or stormy day, I would be on horseback all day, just going into the house to snatch something to eat and out again. If there was anything hard to do Jean could do it. On one occasion I remember we had a lot of wild cows which had never been in a corral before. The excitement of driving them was very great. The peon would go one way, I the other. The animals would come racing and kicking, and sometimes come full force into me and send me flying off my horse. I would laugh at this. It would often take from early dawn until late in the morning before we could get them in. I would often lasso them – I could use a lasso as well as any man. The animals would stray, and in order to find them I would stand on my horse and look through a little glass I had. I could see for miles across the flat camp. It was a common thing for neighbours to ask me, when they met me, if I could tell them anything of their straying animals. I was very well known, loved by some and feared (although I was young) by many, for I would have justice at any cost. Once there was dispute about the measurement of Father's camp, as they said they had measured it and it was not as much as Father claimed. He would have given in, but I stepped it out with my horse and found it was ours by right, and proved it to be so. After that the natives found that if they wanted to cheat they had to deal with me.

I was terribly hurt one day when I overheard Father say to someone how sorry he was that he had no son. I went to him afterwards and said, 'Do I not do the work of a man, and take a son's place? I have always tried to do so.' He took me in his arms and said that I did all a son could do, but that he did not like me having to do a man's work. I was comforted then, for though I worked in this way it did not trouble me, for I was big, healthy and strong. I did not know what it meant to be overtired or exhausted. I have often killed and skinned both sheep and oxen. I mention this to show how strong I was; there was no work on our farm which I could not and did not do when the occasion required it of me.

My parents now took in about seven orphan boys – at any rate, boys who had no one to care for them and look after them. It must be understood that at that time slavery had not been suppressed, and in some instances great cruelty took place, so that when kind people took and cared for these homeless little creatures, it was a great blessing for them.[9] Those boys came under my care. Oh! what wild young things they were, and what a lot of looking after they required. Father had a teacher for them, but when they were outside it was like trying to get wild cattle in, to get them under control and back to the house, so I had a whip, and used it too. Sometimes my sister would come out and call me cruel. The boys would at once turn on her and say it was no business of hers, and I could whip them if I liked.

In after years the same boys, grown to men, have come to me and made themselves known, and many laughs we have had over the old days. Father now bought 400 head of cattle from a Mr. T. five leagues away. He made a large *potrero*[10] (double ditch) and so shut the cattle in at night. One night a dense foggy mist came in, and we found that the peon, whose work it was to collect the animals, had missed more than half, and we knew that in all probability they would have wandered back to their previous owner, but it was no use looking for them till morning. At dawn, Father and Mr. S. went off, telling me to follow as soon as I had finished the milking. As soon as I finished, I jumped on my horse (I had a good one and could make it do anything I wished) and galloped off. Reaching the place, I found our cattle mixed up with others; I could tell them by their head marks. I could see nothing of Father or Mr. S. so I started separating them. (I was generally rather successful at this, for it wants quickness and tact.) I went on for some hours, sometimes in high thistles. At last I got them all back, after being nine hours in the saddle in the boiling sun, and I had not even had a drink of water. When I arrived

9. Slavery had, in fact, been constitutionally abolished in a series of laws passed during 1812 and 1813, although the turbulent political climate made consistent enforcement difficult. By the time Jane refers to, therefore, no children should have lived in fear of being formally enslaved, but practice probably did not match theory, with the result that orphans were still vulnerable to exploitation.

10. Jane's definition of a *potrero* as a 'double-ditch' is puzzling, for this term usually denotes nothing more than a fenced pasture.

home my face and hands were streaming with blood from the scratches and thorns of the thistles. It took Mother some time to remove them all.

When Father returned he said, 'Why did Jean not come? We waited for her at Mr. G.'s where we had breakfast, and then the sun was too strong to start work.' When he found that I had done the work of separating the cattle by myself, in the heat of the sun, he said he could have cried. I said, 'Well, Father, I have cried many times today when I was hot and tired and discouraged.' I felt that by my strength of will I had done much that day, and I said to myself, I will not give in. I think it must have made a great impression on me, for from that time I never allowed myself to say, I cannot do a thing; if I could not manage one way, I would find another.

There grew up between my father and myself a perfect understanding. He put implicit confidence in me, and I was determined to live up to it and give him every reason to trust me. Whatever I did he appeared to know my motive at once, and looking back over the years now, I can say my father understood me better than any other human being ever has.

My sisters and I had some animals of our own. One day a man came to buy some cattle, and we agreed that ours should also be sold, but I wanted to keep one for which I had a great fancy. When the man began to pick the animals he intended taking, my father told him not to take my favourite cow as there was another exactly like it, perhaps a little better. The man, of course, thought mine was the best and that was why I wished to keep it back, so he insisted on taking mine. My cow had the hair cut off short at the tip of the tail, and while the man went in for breakfast I cut the other cows' tails just the same. When he came out to go on with his work he said, 'Which is the cow I have chosen?'. I was feeling so angry with him that I said, 'Just choose now, you see there is no difference.' He did choose and to my delight got the other cow not mine. I felt very pleased with myself – I had won the day and kept my pet cow.

About this time there was to be a grand procession in town, headed by the three Rosas brothers. They were fine looking men. A friend came and said she would like to take Christina and me to see it. I was delighted, needless to say, as more hard work than pleasure came my way, and this was a rare occasion. Mother gave each of us some money, to Christina 20 dollars and to me only 2 dollars. I made no remark but noticed the difference in the amount, and felt that sometimes I was treated as a child but when there was work to be done I had to be a woman. After seeing the procession and the wonders of the city, which to us country-bred girls was very wonderful, we went to look at the shops. Christina spent her money and said to me, 'Now you spend yours', but I refused and said that I did not think it worthwhile. We had a little discussion about it, but I would not give in. When we arrived home I went to Mother and, handing her the two dollars, said, 'Thank you for the money you lent me.' I suppose this was rather sarcastic, but I felt keenly the difference made between the two of us. Mother smiled and said, 'Oh, you little miser.' Father looked up and said, 'Well, dear Jean, I glory in your independent, noble spirit.' This praise was sweet to me, and I have, I think, carried this spirit through life. However much I may have wanted a thing, if I could not provide it for myself I would go without it. I never asked even my parents to give me anything.

Two years after this incident I was thinking of getting married and wanted to provide bedding, etc. I had a good many lambs which I had reared, as the mothers had died. I clipped these and made mattresses of the wool. I also had sixteen young horses of which I was very proud, as I had brought them up entirely by myself. Though we worked hard, there were times of fun, dancing and merriment. On holidays people would come out to us, and often travellers passing through the camp would spend the night with us. This was a very hospitable country. It was understood that no one ever refused hospitality, and it was a nice break to the dullness and sameness of camp life for people to come and tell us all the news.

In the year 1840 I was married to Hugh Robson. He had come out with his parents as a little boy, among the other Colonists, in the good ship 'Symmetry'. I had many good offers, as the world counts them good, but I always resolved I would never marry a man richer than myself. Some would no doubt call this an odd and ridiculous idea. Perhaps it was, but I never regretted it, and my independent spirit had nothing to suffer from this cause. We were married at my father's *estancia*, 'New Caledonia', by Dr. Brown,[11] on February 3rd at 12 o'clock. There was a very large gathering of Scotch friends; we had breakfast at one o'clock and at 3 p.m. we started for our new home, accompanied by Father, Mother and all our guests, a goodly number, and all on horseback.

11. On the life of the Reverend William Brown, see Introduction, p. 10.

I must mention my wedding dress. It was a very fine, white lawn, trimmed with embroidery – a very beautiful dress for those days – and undoubtedly prized by me as it had a history. I have mentioned before the old Irish peon we had when I was a child. He had not only lost his arm, but a great part of the flesh had been torn away from his left side, only leaving the skin over the heart (or so it appeared) which one could see distinctly beating. I often did him little services and he was very devoted to me, and when we were children he never went for his holiday or into town without bringing us some little offering. Some four years before my marriage he asked a mutual friend to buy a dress for me and sent it. I had no use for it just then so put it away carefully, and this was my wedding gown. Poor old fellow, he was a very faithful servant and most grateful for any kindness shown him.

Before leaving my old home my father called me to him and said, 'Jean, you have been a good daughter, I have never lifted my hand to you nor let any other do so; be as good a wife as you have been a daughter; God and his mercy be with you.' He gave me some animals, 10 cows, and, among other things, a cheese press, and said, 'Go Jean, and make your fortune.' He evidently thought I was capable of doing so.

Well now to return to the start for my new home, which was seven leagues away. We all rode along merrily till the last league, when there was a race to see who would get to the house first. There was tremendous excitement, all galloping their hardest, the first one to arrive was to be rewarded by a kiss from the bride. We danced all that night and at sunrise the party prepared to leave, but the fun was not yet quite over. On their return journey each house they came to with a Scotch resident (there were very few), they dismounted and danced and sang, Father and Mother being the leaders. Nearly all the Scotch families were connected in some way with my family, if only by ties of friendship, and are still, in many cases to the fourth generation. The natives, of course, thought the *ingleses* had all gone quite mad, not knowing that this was an old Scotch custom.

Our house was on McC.'s ground, but we soon found that it was too small, so my husband went away to find a more convenient place. That night a tremendous storm came on. I was up rounding and keeping our sheep together. A neighbour had a large flock of sheep which he did not look after properly. I could hear them coming and knew that they would mix with ours, so I called my help, a boy of 10 years old, to look after our sheep while I drove the others towards their home. While I was away the boy had let many of our sheep stray. The next day, when Hugh returned, he went to claim the sheep from the man he knew had them, but could only get part of them back. There was some mean trickery and we had to lose them – and this man was a relative.

The country at this time was again very unsettled, and a revolution broke out in Chascomús, so all the English speaking people went into the city, amongst them my husband's relatives.[12] They tried to persuade me to go also, but I said, 'No, I will remain with my husband and help him, if we must flee we will go together.' Hugh went to help his sister to go to town, and while he was away the revolutionists came and took all our horses, leaving me only one out of sixteen. They took my favourite riding horse, so I followed them for six leagues trying to get my horse back. The captain said he would try and see if it could be returned. After a weary day and a lot of patience I did get my horse, to my keen delight. I was determined to have my favourite back, if perseverance and worrying could do it.

One of the many troubles we had to contend with was the soldiers coming and taking our horses. No one dared refuse them; the only thing to do was to hide them, and this I have done on more than one occasion. I have put my best horses in a bedroom as a place of safety – a queer stable, but in those days one had to do all sorts of things to protect one's property and outwit the army and those in authority. Had I resorted this time to this way of hiding my horse, I should not have had such a tedious long day, following the soldiers and begging that my own property should be returned.

One day my husband and I were working when a peon came rushing up, calling for help. A drunken Irishman had gone to McC.'s and stabbed him. My husband seized a saw and I a stick and we rushed away as hard as we could. When we arrived McC. was lying in a pool of blood in the most terrible condition. He said, 'I am dying.' Between us we got him on to the bed, fearing he would die as we did so, for we did not know how badly he was injured, but I knew he was severely wounded. I was

12. This is a reference to the uprising of October to November 1839 in the southern part of Buenos Aires Province. See Introduction, pp. 33-34.

removing his clothes to find the wound and try to stop the flow of blood when there was a noise behind me at the door, and there was the villain. Not knowing that we had come, he had returned to finish his horrible deed and make sure he had quite killed his victim. My husband sprang at him, and then began a fierce struggle. The man was much bigger and stronger than Hugh, and mad with drink and baffled over his evil intentions. I soon saw that my husband would be overpowered by his fury. As they fell he attempted to get his knife from his back, where they always carry it. I felt I must help or my husband who was underneath would share the same fate as McC. I was holding the wounded man, but leaving him I sprang over them as they were lying on the ground, and seizing the first thing I could find, which was a spade, I held it over his head as if I was going to strike him. This frightened him for an instant, and Hugh managed to get uppermost. I called to the boy to bring some cow ties of raw hide, and I was in the act of bringing this round his body to tie his arms, when he gave me a most vicious kick in my stomach, which sent me reeling against the wall. The pain was very great and for the moment my senses seemed as though they were leaving me, but my determined Scotch blood was up and I dashed forward again, and this time, careful not to put myself in a position where he could kick me, I got one arm bound and then drew the lasso quickly round the other arm, after which we could bind his feet together. He had native spurs on, and he kicked the floor so violently that he smashed them to pieces, strong as they were. Leaving him I then turned to McC., as my husband was quite exhausted and could do nothing for a while. McC. was moaning feebly and whispered, 'It's no good, I am dying.' It was an awful gash, but something must be done, and as I tried to close it I thought there was little hope of saving his life. I then burned some rag, using some of my own garments, and with this I stopped the bleeding. Then I bound him up and did what I could for him. My husband had to leave me to send the boy off for the *alcalde* [local law-officer]. I felt very ill and must have fainted. When I recovered it was a ghastly scene as I had fallen in a pool of blood and was covered with it. Mr. McC. was quite delirious, and the man was cursing and vowing that when he was free, never mind how long it took, he would kill my husband. The *alcalde* came and took the man to prison, and I heard that after a term of prison he was sent on to a ship; no doubt he was kept in order there, and trained. I never heard or saw any more of him, though for many months after, he figured in my dreams each night, and I went over that horrible struggle again and again. McC. happily recovered from his wound, and after a time married an Irish girl, whose mother saw part of the struggle we had with McC.'s would-be murderer. They lived in this same place and I still know and see their children's children.

In 1841 we moved north. We had to cross the Maldonado river on our journey. We had with us some cows and 1,800 sheep, but when we arrived at the banks of the river the sheep would not pass, try as we would; the cows and three carts of luggage went on. I was on horseback helping to drive the sheep; it took us five hours to get those sheep over. This delayed us so much that night came on. We went on our way until ten o'clock when the moon went down, so there was nothing to do but wait till daybreak. It was the end of May, and very cold with sharp frost. We unsaddled, after having been riding for 18 hours, and I lay down with my saddle for a pillow. My brother covered me with his *recado*[13] – for I had no wrap of any kind – as I had imagined we should reach our destination well before nightfall. I was so weary that, in spite of my hard bed, I slept. The next morning we started at daybreak. I was not well at the time and felt quite ill and unfit to face the heavy work before me.

In August my first child was born, a son. We remained two years at this place, and a terrible two years it was. Our stock was attacked by leech and we lost everything. One of the most awful storms that I ever remember having seen in my long experience of this country's severe storms, occurred in January 1842. The wind took everything before it; our sheep travelled many leagues, literally carried by the storm. Of course, we lost the greater part of them. One man estimated that his sheep had been carried by the wind for about 30 leagues. As he was returning from following them his horse fell dead under him from fatigue and cold. My husband, seeing the man, brought him into our house. He was almost frozen and it was some time before he could get warm, and this was

13. *recado*: a flexible, sheepskin-covered saddle favoured by the gaucho. For a detailed description of the gaucho's riding equipment, see Fernando O. Assunçao, *El gaucho*, 2 vols (Montevideo: Dirección General de Extensión Universitaria, 1978), II, 157-214. On the *recado*, see pp. 173-96. Alternatively, see Richard W. Slatta, *Gauchos and the Vanishing Frontier* (Lincoln, Nebraska, and London: University of Nebraska Press, 1983), pp. 72-75.

during the hottest part of the year; it was a very curious and unusual storm. I have often experienced intense cold in the early morning before the sun gains power, but as it rises higher the heat is always very great. It is lovely in the camp in the spring when the sun rises and all is fresh and green.

On one of our moves, there was a lot to be done when we arrived, and I was working away putting up a shelter which was built principally of a sort of grass or reed. I had to keep going up and down the ladder, which was very tiring. I was not strong at the time, and was feeling overwrought. Presently a man came along – a man whom I felt would not do me a good turn – but I imagined that upon seeing a woman working, he might help me a little, so I asked him if he would hand up some of the reeds, but he simply laughed and refused. I felt so angry that I said something I would not have said at any other time. I said, 'For this may you die in the camp like a dog, with no one to help you in your time of need.' I felt at once that I ought not to have said it, for somehow these predictions of mine do come true, as it did in this case, for the man died out in the camp in a ditch.

In 1843 we came to 'Los Sauces', T. R.'s, where we had 21,000 sheep on thirds and also a large dairy. My life seems to be made up of fresh starts after failures; it wanted a strong heart to battle with it. I had to work night and day, for at night there were the animals to look after and collect, housework, sewing and washing to do, for I had no woman to help me. We had, of course, peones for the outside work, but they were so untrustworthy and would go off on a drinking bout or amuse themselves in their own fashion and were so much trouble to look after, that they were worse than useless.

This period was the time of the French and English blockade, and all imported things were at fabulous prices, indeed, all living was very expensive, tea at 10 dollars a pound, salt 6 dollars a pound.[14] This made it very difficult for us to make ends meet, though I worked as perhaps no woman has ever done – I even killed animals for our meat.

One day I was out riding when my horse caught his foot in a *vizcacha's*[15] hole and nearly fell. With a tremendous effort I pulled

14. Here Jane refers to the joint naval blockade of Buenos Aires implemented by Britain and France from 1845 to 1848. See Introduction, pp. 14–15.
15. *vizcacha*: a small, rabbit-like rodent which dwells in burrows. The *vizcacha's* tunnels pose a serious hazard to travellers on horseback, for they undermine the ground and are difficult to spot.

him up, but in doing so I hurt my back very badly and before I recovered from that my second baby was born. I was very, very ill. My husband went off to fetch my mother, but did not find her at home, and had many leagues to go before he could get a woman to come to me. Six hours elapsed before he returned. I was quite alone, except for my little three year old son.

With my little dead baby beside me, I made a vow to my God that if I were spared to do so, I would go to any woman in a similar situation, never mind who it was or how far away. I have kept that vow and many are the times that I have been called upon to fulfil it. In those undertakings I have always asked my God to be with me and help me, and I know he has, as I have often felt that he was very close to me. I have often been called to go to some sick person, and started off on a dark and sometimes stormy night and ridden from five to ten leagues. In the camp in those days there was no doctor, and as the *ranchos* [dwellings] were so far apart, women (and others too) had to suffer greatly, and but for the help of those who were near enough and could, or would, go to them, they came off very badly. I became quite used to being Doctor as well as nurse, and many daring things I did, things that had to be done on the instant, with a life at stake. Our remedies were most primitive, but I really think they were as good and effectual as the scientific ones of later days. I always think that having attended and doctored animals as a child and also having studied nature has taught me many lessons which I have found work with human beings. As I have said, when my baby was born I registered a vow that I would always help when I could, and I was very soon called upon to do so. I was asked to attend to a Mrs. B. and very ill she was, poor thing. I was only a young woman then and this was my first patient. I cannot remember the numbers I have attended to in the years that have passed. Some were very poor and had nothing for sickness at hand. I have often torn and used the clothes I was wearing to supply some urgent need. I gained a sort of reputation that my patients recovered where there seemed little hope. It may have been a case of faith healing, the power of mind over body.

I had been married some four years and had a young sister staying with me. I had to go some leagues across the camp on business, so I took my sister behind me on my horse and my little child on my knee. We cantered along for some distance seeing nothing to alarm us, as one could see a great distance across the wide flat camp. Presently I happened to look round and saw a horseman, and from that distance he looked a rough looking fellow. I took no notice at first but increased my pace a little, then I found he did the same and it was evident that he was trying to overtake me. I whipped up my horse, and then it became a hard race. My sister was very frightened and kept telling me how he was gaining on us, and for a time he seemed to be. We raced like this for about a league, and then I saw a ranch and rode towards it and pulled up, thinking the man would go off as he might suppose I was remaining there, but I did not intend going in as probably there would be no one at home. I gave my horse time to get his breath and then started again. My horse was swift and strong and was as excited as we were, and galloped hard without stopping for a long distance. Just as the man was gaining on us we came to the house for which I was bound. We rushed in headlong and I was able to bang the door in his face. Today this must all seem ridiculous; why did we imagine the man meant mischief? but at the time the taking of life and property was held very lightly, and theft or even murder was committed just to gain a few dollars.

Around 1845 my husband and I were with a wedding party. The bridegroom was my husband's brother. All the party was on horseback, on their way to the newly married couple's home. We had travelled a long way and we all felt very thirsty. Passing a *pulpería* [the typical bar-cum-grocery store of the pampas], we stopped, and the man seeing we were a wedding party did not bring just a glass of what each one ordered, but the whole bottle. When we had finished my husband insisted on paying. The man charged for the whole bottle, although there was only one small glass taken out of most of them. There was lemonade, brandy, whisky, *caña* [sugar-cane spirit] and *horchata* [a typically Spanish non-alcoholic drink made from ground tiger nuts, not usually associated with Argentina]. After the bill had been paid the man took the bottles inside. I followed him inside and said, 'Are all the bottles paid for?'. He said, yes. 'Very well', I said, and seizing one in each hand I proceeded to water the floor with the contents. After emptying them all, to the intense disgust of the man, I told him that perhaps it might teach him to be honest next time and only charge for the amount drunk. The flies would now give him something to do, as the sweet stuff on the floor would attract them by the thousands. It was much better that they should benefit by it than this dishonest man. Needless to say, this caused the rest of the party much amusement and there was great laughter.

Now I come to about the year 1853. A man and his wife and child came to us one day and begged us to take them in. They had come out from town to stay with some relatives, but some misunderstanding arose and they parted. I felt sorry for them and took them in as the woman was unfit to travel. Four days after they arrived a baby was born, and I nursed it and looked after the mother. Time went on and they remained with us for six months, and we treated them as one of the family. What I am about to relate will show how they repaid us. We had been milking a great many cows, and making a lot of butter and cheese, in fact we had been doing very well and had saved a good deal of money, and we intended buying some land. I had put this money away in a chest for the time being. The man and woman knew of this hiding place, in fact they knew all that went on in the house, most unfortunately as it turned out for us.

One day I was going into Chascomús with my husband to take cheese and butter for sale. I had mounted my horse and was just starting off when I found it was very cold, so I returned to the house again and taking my baby, who was six weeks old (my boy John) up in his cradle, I carried him from my bedroom into the dining room, and threw a heavy coat over the cradle; on thinking about it afterwards, I could not imagine why I had done so, but thank God I was led to do it. I fastened the doors, leaving the other children out at play, and, knowing I should not be absent very long, I left, feeling that no harm could come to them. We went into Chascomús and sold our cheeses, etc. When about half way home, on our return, I saw a black cloud just over where our house should be. I said to my husband, 'What a curious cloud', and then I exclaimed, 'My God, it must be our house.' While I spoke I thought I could see flames. I knew then that my fears were correct. I had a whale bone whip and I lashed my horse so furiously that soon there was little of the whip left. Oh, what a mad gallop that was, each instant seemed an age. On I flew, my good horse going his hardest. All the time I was picturing my little helpless baby in that burning house, as I knew the other children could run from the flames. Any mother must recognise the agony I was enduring.

At last I was in sight of the burning mass. The children on seeing me came running and close behind them a man whom I thought was a stranger. In his arms he had my baby. I threw myself from my horse and snatching my little one to me I felt overpowered with joy and thankfulness. But this was not the time to give way to my feelings. I reverently thanked my God from a heart full of gratitude that he had spared my baby, and putting the little one in the ditch, I ran to the burning house hoping that I might save some part of it, but it was hopeless; it was a mass of flames and nothing could be done. Here was a trial of faith. I had helped that man and his wife to the utmost of my power, and they had rewarded me by robbing my house and so that it should not be discovered had set it on fire and departed. I was loath to believe such base ingratitude, but it was so. In no other way could the house have taken fire except by some person deliberately causing it, as at that time there were no matches and only flint and steel were used to obtain a light, so no small child could do it. How differently the man who had saved my child returned a kindness I had once done him. I will now tell you about it.

Two years previously a man came to our house one day and begged us to help him, as the authorities were looking for him to make him serve in the army. I told him we were surrounded by soldiers who were helping with the shearing, and that it would not be safe either for him or ourselves to have him in the house. Then I thought of a shelter there was outside, and for three days I hid him there and took him his food. On the third night he rode away and we did not see him until two years after. He was passing and saw the flames, and thinking the house was quite empty he attempted to put out the fire. Getting on the roof he beat it till the thatch gave way, and then he discovered the baby. The fire was burning furiously in the room from which I had removed the baby. He forced the door open at last and got into the dining room and found the cradle just on fire. He pulled the baby out quite uninjured; the heavy coat which I had thrown over the cradle had saved it from catching fire at once, though the part which was unprotected was burned. The man took the baby and the cradle out (the same cradle one of my daughters still has and has used for all her children; it is a precious possession in the family). The first time the man came to our house, I saved him from a very unhappy fate, the next time he came he saved my child's life. When I cast my bread upon the waters, little did I think that it would return to me in such a manner. The man left and I have never seen him again, though I have often wished I could have shown him my gratitude. Only the part of the house composed of bricks was left standing, so all the rest had to be rebuilt.

We lived there for some years. Years of sorrow and happiness, for I found much joy in my growing family. My little boy James (he was about six years old) was very fond of catching and riding spirited horses. One day one of these ran away with him and threw him, poor little man; I saw it happen. He came to me and I tried to find out if he was hurt, but he did not seem to be or child-like he did not complain. In a day or two he began to fail and then became very ill. I did what I could and then sent for the doctor. When he came he said that my poor little boy was injured internally and nothing could be done. After some days of great pain, little James passed away. We took our boy into town and buried him in the English cemetery. I was very grieved over my son's death and felt that I could not endure much more sorrow, but there was trouble awaiting me on my return. I found that the *estancia*, on which we had just spent a great deal of money in order to improve it, had been sold over our heads to a man I had helped – for whom I had done a lot.[16] When his wife heard about it she said that she would be very angry with him if he did take it from us, so he said he would give it up. I was feeling very sore about the whole matter, and unsettled too, and was determined to look for fresh camp so that there would be no chance of it being sold. I must tell of a journey I had, seeking this camp, with my little son Hugh as a companion. We started at sunrise and rode for many leagues. We had to cross the Samborombón river,[17] which was getting high and there was a lot of water in the camp, but at the place we passed, the horses could cross without swimming. Well, I looked at the camp I thought of buying, and practically decided to take it. On our return journey it got very stormy and a tremendous wind started blowing, which we had to face. We battled along, thinking that after we had crossed the river we had not far to go. We made for the part I thought best, but imagine my dismay – weary, hungry and night time coming on – to find it quite impossible to

16. The sale of the Robsons' home without their consent indicates, presumably, that it was built on land rented without the assurance of any proper leasing agreement.

17. *Samborombón river*: waterway originating to the north-west of the town of Chascomús, running approximately south-eastwards into Samborombón Bay.

cross. I said to my boy, 'We must try somewhere farther down.' We struggled on and at last I thought I could see smoke, that meant a habitation of some sort and human beings. We made for it and found a man there. He told us we must go to a place some six leagues further down the river before it was safe to cross, and kindly said he would show us the way. When we reached the spot it looked terrible, the water was rushing along, and my boy said, 'Oh Mother, we cannot go over here, I feel so frightened and I have such a little horse that the water will come over me.' I said, 'Oh no, you keep close by me and your horse will swim high, you will be quite safe.' He had on a jersey which I thought I could seize and hold him up if necessary. We plunged in and waded a little distance, but the current was so strong and the water so deep that our horses were soon off their feet and were swimming. It was not a pleasant experience as we were very tired. Reaching the other side we had to go back the same distance we had come along the river bank. By this time it was quite dark and I had only the stars to guide me, and they were not very clear. I knew there should be a house about somewhere, and so there was for we soon saw a faint light and made for it. I clapped my hands and a man and a woman appeared. I asked for shelter and rest. The man said, 'Why, you must be a Rodger.' He came towards me and said, 'Come in.' I said, 'You must help me for I am so stiff that I cannot get off my horse.' So he and his wife helped me to get off my horse and carried me into the house. It was some time before I could move, for I was so numb and stiff from being so long in the saddle, and wet through besides, that my limbs seemed partially paralysed. The man then turned to Hugh and said, 'Get off, and come in', but, poor little boy, he was in the same condition that I was, and was utterly incapable of moving alone. These kind people took us in, gave us dry clothing, warm drinks and refreshment, and made a big fire by which to dry our clothes. After a rest we were able to go on our way, and very grateful we were for this help in time of need.

Some time after this journey, I sold ten cows to a man. He was unable to pay the money down at the time but said he would be shearing shortly and that after selling the wool he would pay me. A month elapsed, and then someone came and told us that the man had sold his wool and gone off to some other part of the country with his family, and that he had already been gone three days on his journey. I said to my husband, 'I will follow him and claim my money.' He said, 'It is no use trying to catch him, if it is true that he has had three days start.' I went first to Chascomús with butter and cheese, and found the rumour was true, so I returned home and taking my son John with me I told my daughter to tell her father what I intended doing and so started on my seemingly rather hopeless journey. However, after riding hard we caught the runaway man and his family just stopping for the night. When the man saw me he was in a state of fright, and immediately began saying he had left the money for me with a friend, which I told him was false. When he found I was not to be put off, he gave me the money. By this time it was quite dark and my boy was rather nervous, for he said, 'Now, Mother, what can we do? This is strange camp.' I said, 'Don't fear, we will keep to the track as long as there is any, and afterwards we will travel by the stars, or trust to Mr. Buchanan's horses as they will make for home' (for we had left our tired horses at Mr. Buchanan's, and he had lent us others). We reached Mr. Buchanan's safely at midnight, and they gave us tea and refreshments. After a little rest and talk we proceeded on our journey homewards, reaching the *estancia* soon after sunrise. I had ridden close on 40 leagues in that day – or rather day and night – only resting that short time at Mr. Buchanan's, and I had used three horses to do it.

In 1857, our church, St. Andrew's, was opened by the Rev. J. Smith, D.D.[18] It was very wet and had been so for many days previously; the camp was in a very bad state for driving. We had a large carriage and a great many of us went, but at times it seemed doubtful if we would manage to get to the Church at all. We had nine leagues to travel, *pantanos* to cross, and sometimes it seemed impossible for us to proceed, even with the many strong horses we had. However, with patience and much bumping and rough tossings, we at last arrived. It was worth the trouble, as we were one and all interested in the ceremony we had come to witness, for at last we had our Church. It had cost us some trouble, I suppose, and we all had in one way or another to deny ourselves something. I think we all felt it was worth it on this day, when our Church was completed, and we had met to rejoice, and knew it was a good work well done.

---

18. On the establishment of this church, see Introduction, pp. 31-32. The Reverend James Smith succeeded the Reverend William Brown after the latter's retirement to Scotland.

In the year 1860 a man came to live next to us, and caused us much trouble. He would steal horses and cattle to change the mark, and would also steal the newly born lambs, and would stop at no mean act. One day my son John came to me and said, 'Mother, I am sure D. has stolen our animals, I can see the hide in his ranch; he and his companions are away, and I looked in.' I said, 'Saddle my horse and I will go and see', as I was determined this time to find out for myself and make an example of him, for these thefts had gone on long enough. Telling John to call his father and ask him to fetch the *alcalde*, I went to D.'s ranch. He was just coming towards it. I went up to him and said, 'You have a skin of ours which you have stolen.' He, of course, began to deny it, and then to use bad language. I said, 'We have sent for the *alcalde*, and he will decide if you are a thief, and what is to be done with you.' He at once changed and began saying, 'Oh, you are a good woman and would not harm a poor Irish boy.' I said, 'You are young, and I think it a pity you should be a thief and lead this dishonest life; we will try and make an honest man of you.' At this he flew at me with some shears he had stuck in his belt. I drew my horse back a few steps, and then turning with my whip in my hand (it was a whale bone one with a lead handle), I said, 'Stand back or I will not answer for your life, and don't think I am alone, for someone is watching.' It was only my daughter but he thought it was a man. He then started pleading again, and said, 'I will give you a thousand dollars if you let this pass.' 'No', I said, 'for then I should be as bad as you are.' He then became desperate, and rushing into the house he came out again with a pistol, and jumping on to his horse which was close at hand was about to make off. I called out, 'Stop!'. He drew his pistol and pointed it at me. I gave my horse a kick and he made one bound alongside the man. My horse was a racer and well trained, knew what was expected of him and answered to my wishes. He threw all his weight against D.'s horse, and at the same instant I grasped D.'s pistol with my left hand and with my elbow in his chest and my foot on his horse's side (he had a small animal) I had complete power, and my hand was as strong as his. There we were, swaying and turning round and round. If I found he was getting the least power, I pressed my foot with all my weight into his horse's side, or rather kidneys, and it would sink down. My horse, thinking it was a race, would lean his whole weight against D.'s horse. The *alcalde* now appeared. As we were struggling we had neared D.'s ranch, and he slipped off his horse and made for it as his came coming out [*sic*]. I called, 'Don't try to get away, it will be worse for you.' My husband and the *alcalde* now came up, and to my great disgust, after all I had gone through to secure him, simply let him go free, so that he left this part of the country. We saw nothing of him for 15 years, when he returned with his brother, who was as disreputable as himself. They again settled down close to us and once more caused great disturbance. They were two men who fought against each other and us, and the two D.'s were made of cat's-paws [were light-fingered]. For some years we had to keep a perpetual and careful watch on our cattle and property, and even then it cost us much annoyance and expense.

I have given the serious side of my life rather than the gay, though we had bright times mixed in with hard work. There is not much amusement in this country, except perhaps dancing, and that is done very often and it gives much enjoyment. My eldest son and my daughter E.'s birthday came within two days of each other, so they were kept up together. We used to have a gathering during the day, with sports, and in the evening we finished off with a dance. We were expecting my son Hugh on his birthday. He did not come as early as we expected, and my little boy John commenced to worry and think he would not come, as I had told them all that if Hugh did not arrive we would not have the dance. However, he did come, and John was in the highest spirits. I don't know why, but often in the midst of gaiety I have on more than one occasion had a foreboding of trouble. I had it now, and do as I would to cast it off I was quite unable to do so. John came to me and saw at once that there was something troubling me. He said, 'Mother, what is it? Are you sad because Jean is leaving you? I will take care of you; come now Mother, and see how I can take the ring.' They were running the *sortija*[19] and he had carried off the ring three times; he was bounding about and leading the fun. Then came dancing and singing, and John sang the song with the words, 'Oh, say it is not here, the father calls thee home.' How often that song has returned to me, and how it made me feel when my dear lad sang it. After the dance our friends went home, only the family remaining, and the next day being Sunday, we were all going to Church. In the morning

19. The pastime of *sortija* enjoyed much popularity among the gauchos. The object of the game was to pass a lance through a small ring suspended from an archway while riding past at full speed.

everybody was preparing to start for Church, some driving, others riding. John came to me with a gun and said, 'Mother, how do I load this?'. I said go to Mr. C. he will tell you, then I said, 'No, one hole will do.' I helped him to load it, little thinking at the time what was to happen. Just then someone came to me and asked me to go to Mrs. R. who was very ill, so I left, and my daughter said to John, 'You come and ride with me', but he said no, that he was not going to Church. This was most unusual as he always liked going, but this day he wanted to go with S., who had a new gun to try.

There had been a lot of rain and there was a lot of water in the camp. The boys took a tub and were punting about, and in doing so the tub upset and they fell into the water – guns and all getting wet. S. was trying to see if his gun would go off, but found it would not, so John said, 'Then mine is useless also, we will go home.' There was a boy in the garden, John and he started laughing and playing together, when a peon passed along and taking up John's gun he said, 'Take care I will shoot you both', and pointing it at them in fun, he pulled the trigger, when to his horror it went off. The shot passed over the lad's head but it struck my boy in the temple. He fell forward not uttering a sound. Oh, my God, how it came back to me afterwards, for I had helped him to load the gun with which he was shot, as the boys had not used the gun at all. I have already said I was at Mrs. R.'s. Suddenly I was alarmed by a boy calling and screaming, 'Mrs. Robson, John has been shot!'. I did not wait even an instant for an explanation, but dragging the boy from the horse he was on I leapt on it, bareback as it was, and I urged it to gallop back home as fast as it could. The R.'s came out, to see me tearing away and clinging to the horse's neck. They thought I was mad, and so I was, with terror. In this way I travelled two miles. How I did it I never knew nor how long it took. I was only conscious of travelling and finding my dear boy in a pool of blood when I arrived. I cried, 'My boy, my boy.' He looked at me and his breast rose three times but he was unable to speak. I bathed his dear face and head. He lived just four hours, then passed away to his God. He alone knew the trial I was passing through, my boy taken from me, my great comfort and joy. He was such a good, gentle lad, always ready to carry out my wishes, and I had thought how soon he would be able to ease me of much responsibility. But it was not to be, and at the time it was hard to think it was for the best. My husband and daughter returned from Church to find this awful tragedy.

I cannot really remember what happened till my husband and daughter came and took me to Mrs. R., who had come to our house to see what had happened. An hour later her baby was born, and in looking after and attending to her, I was unable to give way to my own grief as I had to think of another. No doubt it was good for me, and in a way saved my reason, for, strong as I was, this shock nearly overcame me. The peon who had done the dreadful deed was told to go away, and never let either myself or family see him again. Some said they would have imprisoned him, but I knew he did not intend to hurt my boy. It was an accident. It proves how wrong it is to play with firearms, even if they are supposed to be unloaded. Mrs. R. was very ill, and caused me great anxiety in nursing her. The baby died, and I went with Hugh and J. and took the little thing into town. It was a terrible journey. At this time – 1868 – there was no burial ground in Chascomús, so we had to cross the Samborombón river. It was very swollen and the camps were full of water. At first we thought it would be impossible to cross, but, with our horses swimming in parts, we managed to reach the other side. It seemed as if one sad thing came on the heels of another, and I was kept busy going from friend to friend (not always friends either). I was helping Mrs. R. when a black woman, her servant, got a terrible gash in her side and was in agony. I believe it was done in a quarrel. They called me and when I saw the gash, two inches long, I thought it beyond my powers to do anything, so after I had bathed the wound I stitched it up with a silk thread and the next day she was taken into town (Buenos Aires). I was told afterwards, I had done my part of the doctoring so well that they let it remain and the woman recovered. Very shortly after this I was again called upon to be a Doctor. A peon was the worse for drink, and fell from his horse on to a bottle he was carrying. It broke, and cut his head very badly. When I came to bathe his head I found that numerous pieces of glass had cut right in. With the point of a knife I managed to remove all the splinters – it was not a nice task. It was a good thing that I had strong nerves, for they were constantly being taxed to the utmost.

I have not mentioned that with the passing of the years, we had gradually bought a good deal of land around our house. For some time past things had not been quite so hard, and though I still kept control over the work, my duties were not so numerous. The country was a little more prosperous, though, alas, revolutions and disturbances still went on. I may mention that at this time no one thought of wearing blue as it was the rebels' colour, red being Rosas's colour. Well, my husband and I were going to ride some leagues to Church. I put on a blue dress, the only one I had then, I thought, suitable to wear. My husband said, 'Jean, don't think of wearing that dress, it is blue and not safe to do so, and you know we have to pass through the encampment of Rosas's soldiers.' I said, 'I am not afraid', but I knew all the time it was a risk, though as usual I would not see fear. We started, and after riding some distance we had to pass through the encampment of Rosas's soldiers which my husband mentioned. We had been riding briskly but pulled up to a walk. I did wonder then what effect my blue dress would have. My husband was nervous and said, 'Now what will we do?'. 'Do?' I said, 'Nothing, just ride on.' They looked at us and we saluted them. They did not attempt to stop us and they saw we were not alarmed. I must say I was a little relieved. From experience I always found it was best to put on a bold front with these gallant warriors. When we reached the house to which we went before Church, they were horrified to see me in my blue gown and begged me not to wear it again, but to buy another one.

I have just remembered about a ride I had into town. My husband was away, and I had to go in on very important business, my only companion being a man I did not altogether trust. Still, it was a case of having his company or going alone. I did not fear that he would harm me, but I had a good deal of money and a watch of my husband's tied up in a bundle. It was a very windy day and it was very hard work riding against it, at times I had to hold my skirt. The man asked me several times to let him carry the bundle for me. I refused, but at last I gave in and gave it to him, thinking that he could not do much as we were riding abreast, and my horse was a better and stronger one than his if he attempted to make off. Well, after a very trying ride of seven leagues we reached town and I went to a friend's house, while the man put up the horses. Then I asked him to go and do some business for me, giving him a hundred dollars with which to pay, as I had to go another way. I was very anxious to return home that day, and so wanted to get through my business quickly, which was unpleasant. I finished what I had to do and returned to my friend's, expecting to find the man there and waiting for me, but no, he had not come. Then I remembered that I had to get the watch mended, went to my parcel, and found the watch gone. Then I thought that the man had probably slipped it out as we rode along, and so it proved, he had not only taken that but had made off with the money I gave him. I waited and hoped he might return but at last it became so late that I had to go. I not only grieved the loss of the money, but the ingratitude of the man for we had done much for him. He went off to Montevideo, and I heard afterwards that he was very sorry he had treated me in that way. He said he had done many mean actions but none he regretted so much as his wicked behaviour to me. It was, I suppose, a sudden temptation to a man who had no moral courage to resist it.

Just as I was starting on my homeward journey I met a young lad who was driving to his home, and for some leagues our road lay in the same direction, so I asked him to let me ride with him for company. We rode until 10 p.m., and when we reached his mother's house he said to me, 'Come in Mrs. Robson and get some refreshment and a rest', but I knew his mother was no friend of mine so I said, 'No, thank you.' He then said, 'I will get you a cup of tea and someone to ride with you, or I will come.' Imagine my feelings when I heard the woman refuse me even this hospitality, though her own son had told her he was ashamed of her. I felt this unkindness intensely. I went on my way home, feeling very sad and weary, with a small boy to accompany me. I had befriended this woman in great need, and she repaid me with this ingratitude.

Time had gone on and there was no need for me to work as hard as formerly, but I was always busy and found pleasure in work, which perhaps many would say was unnecessary, but if there was work to be done I felt I must do it.

Several of us went to the races one day. I remember this particular occasion very well as it was St. Patrick's day. There was ladies' side saddle races to be run, for a prize. My husband and I, with a young sister, and several others, set off in good spirits for we expected some fun and some interesting races. Well, some of the races were run and then it came to one between an Irishman and a native. They both had good hopes of winning and ran almost evenly. Just as they were coming to the winning post they both made a mistake and ran the wrong side of the boundary flags. The Irishman was first, but for some reason best known to themselves, the judges decided in favour of the native. At once, of course, there was a great discussion, some taking one side and some the other. I felt sure there would be a row. The Irishman had a young brother with him who had just come out to the country, and knew nothing of the character of the natives. Seeing the winner (the native) going off, he ran after him and seized him by the leg. Just as I reached him the native made a swipe at him with his knife, cutting his face. I then stood in front of him (while the soldiers who were supposed to be keeping order had not yet arrived on the scene). Two or three now tried to get at the boy, pulling me from side to side and stabbing at the boy under my arms. They would not hurt me, I knew, for I was on good terms with the natives. At last it got too much for me, for it had now become a free fight, so I called out to the English, 'Are you going to see your countryman butchered?'. Then they came. The Irishman who had been racing was now mixed up with the rest and a man attacked him. He put up his hand to defend himself, and his brutal assailant made a cut at him, slashing two fingers completely off and sending them flying through the air, and two others were cut through and just hanging. We were now surrounded by English people and they protected us while I got on my horse and took the wounded man on behind. I bound his wounded hand up in my large neck handkerchief and rode off with him to our house. We had no sooner got in safely when I saw the *alcalde* and two soldiers coming. I went to the door and stood with a hand on either side waiting for them. They came with much bluster and said they had come for the man and would take him away bound like a pig. I said, 'You will not have him and don't dare to put a foot in my house. The man is seriously wounded; if you took him and he died, his death would be at your door. I will be responsible for him appearing before the Justice.' With that, after some more argument, they left. They kept our English friends in prison for two days, though they had really done nothing. On the second day they informed me I was to appear with my man. On my way in I took him to a doctor, who said he dare not do anything till after the man had been tried. On we went, and I got the first hearing, fortunately for me, and much to the disgust of the *alcalde*, who wanted to give his version of the affair. He had been delayed by a dispute with his English prisoners, who refused to be driven in front like cattle, but said they would follow. When he finally arrived, the Justice told him he had heard the true facts and that the man was not to blame and he was allowed to go free. The *alcalde* was furious, and after this he never lost a chance of doing us harm if he could. I was very glad I came off best, for the poor man had suffered enough by losing his fingers, and if he had been imprisoned as well it would have been hard indeed. That day we had started for the races and a little innocent amusement and it had ended with this horrid incident.

There was an old lady named Mrs. C. living not far from our *estancia*. I had known her all my life for she came out with us [on the *Symmetry*]. She was taken very ill and, after a time, died. I felt very sorry when I heard that they thought of burying her in the camp (for we had no burial ground in Chascomús in those days – none nearer than Buenos Aires). I said to my husband, 'We must take her into town.' He said, 'We cannot do that, the horses are so thin that they could not do the journey.' This was true as we had a long drought and there was no fodder for the animals. Now they had started the railway and the trucks were running along the line as far as Chascomús. A Mr. P. who knew the contractors said he would ask them to take the body on a truck. We put the coffin in a wagon driven by a man; Mr. P. went on horseback and my husband and I were driving. In this way we crossed the camp for some way. When we got to the Samborombón river the horses in the wagon refused to cross. This delayed us a bit, so I said to my husband, 'You go and help the others and I will drive in front with our horses (as our horses did not refuse to cross) and the other horses will probably follow', which they did quite well. Soon after, we came in sight of the newly made railway, and I saw in the distance that an engine and some trucks were about to start. I stood up and waved my handkerchief to attract their attention. They stopped for us, and when we explained what we wanted they at once very kindly agreed to take us. We got safely into town and took the corpse to a friend's house for that night, and the next day we went to the English cemetery where good Dr. Smith, lovingly called 'Padre', read the service, and we left our old friend Mrs. C. in the peaceful little English cemetery.

In 1867 my daughter Mary was married at the *estancia* 'Esperanza'. We had a very gay wedding, a lot of friends and relations coming from town. In the evening we finished up with a dance and all went very merrily. In one large room the elder ones were dancing, while in another the children were playing, romping and enjoying themselves in their own way. There was a large lamp in the children's room which was thrown over and smashed – how it happened no one seemed to know. I heard the crash and rushed in to find the flames going up almost to the ceiling. At once there was great confusion. The gentlemen ran for water, but I knew that was worse than useless. Running into my bedroom I seized the mattress. There was a little baby comfortably asleep on the bed, but I just rolled it, clothes and all, to one side. I ran back into the room and was just going to fling the mattress on to the flames when some of them dragged me back, probably fearing that I would do myself some harm. I was very angry for the fire was gaining some hold. I wrenched myself free and again seized the mattress and threw it on the flames. In doing so, I fell forward myself, but fortunately I was up again instantly and was not hurt. The fire was extinguished, and not much harm done after all, but it was a funny sight to see the gentlemen all running about with buckets of water in their white kid gloves. I wonder why it did not occur to them that it was useless to throw water on burning oil. Our fright was soon over, and I don't think we took it as a bad omen for the newly wedded happy pair.

In those days we had no post and the only means we had of sending and receiving letters was by a messenger on horseback. As my family was becoming scattered, I felt this very much when I wanted to get news from some of them and it was impossible to do so. One day I was expecting my son Hugh to come and bring me news of my brother, who was living in Chascomús. All the previous day I had a sad foreboding and felt something was going to happen of a distressing nature. At night I had a strange dream. I dreamt I was trying to find my brother and kept asking if anyone could tell me where he was. Then I found myself in a yard and kept going round and round looking for him. It was a yard I had never seen before. When I awoke I was still thinking of my brother, and wondering if anything was wrong. My son Hugh arrived in the evening and seeing I was worried about something, he thought it best to tell his father the bad news he had. It was that in passing through Chascomús he had seen his uncle and he was very ill. My husband knew it was best to tell me, and said, 'We must start early the next morning to see him.' We started at sunrise, and when we arrived in Chascomús I saw the very yard of which I had been dreaming (at the time I did not know just where my brother was living) and this same yard was pointed out to me as being the place where he was living. It came as a shock to me. I dismounted from my horse and hurried in and was met by a woman. I said, 'I have come to see my brother.' She said, 'You cannot do that for he is dead and already in his coffin.' I felt very sad, for my brother was dear to me; he was our only brother and very much loved by us all. We took the dear boy into the

English cemetery. In this country such a very short time is allowed between death and burial. So many times I have been to this burial ground with dear ones; it is so pretty and nicely kept.

On our return home I found that Mrs. R. was very ill and I had been asked to go to her, so without even taking the dust off me I started off again. For ten days I nursed her, and then felt she needed other advice than the doctor who was attending to her, as he said that if her bodily health improved, her mind would never be strong again. I had some trouble in persuading her father to allow me to take her into town, though her husband was anxious to do so. When he did give his consent, in a few minutes we had her in a coach and left. We arrived at the British Hospital. I went in first, and to my astonishment and disgust the Doctor informed me the hospital was not for women but only for men, and that he could not receive Mrs. R. I said he must, or I would tell everybody that they had refused to take in a sick woman when brought to the doors of the hospital, and what would the public think if I had to take her to a Spanish hospital? The Scottish and Irish people had collected money for 14 years for this hospital, and now they refused to take a sick woman in. The doctor then said he would take her but that it would be at his own risk, as he did not know what unpleasantness might arise and how his action might be questioned. We took her into a room, and her sister and I remained to nurse her, for there were no women nurses and this was the first woman patient that had been taken into the British Hospital. From that time to the present both sexes were received. After about a month Mrs. R. was able to leave, quite cured, and could again take up her home duties, so through my persistence I was the means of this hospital taking female patients.

One hears that the wheels of the law move slowly, and in this country I have experienced it more often than I care to think; besides which it is an expensive luxury. I can laugh now (though at the time it was anything but a laughing matter) when I think of a time in which I was kept waiting and waiting for a paper to be signed. At last I determined to close matters one way or another, and so decided to beard the lawyer in his den though I had been told that no woman went to an office where law matters were settled. I remarked, 'It is a funny place that women could not go.' When I arrived at the office I first came to a room where there were a lot of men waiting, and I could see through a door into an inner room where the

Judge was engaged with a man. As soon as I saw the man prepare to leave, I walked in and demanded the great man's attention to my business. He at once made excuses and said he had not my paper there. I turned, and among a whole lot on the table I saw my paper and recognised the signature. I pulled it out and confronted him with it. He was very angry and talked a great deal, but I came off victorious for he signed the paper. I think he was glad to do so and be rid of me. I did not mind that; I had gained my point and was able to return to my home. As I was on my way to the lawyer's office, a man who had really been the chief culprit in causing me a great deal of annoyance, made a rude remark and jeered at me as I passed. I said nothing, but the thought passed my mind, 'May you fall down dead.' It was banished from my mind as quickly as it came. I am thankful it did as things turned out. Someone came to me as I returned from business an hour later and told me that this man had fallen down dead where he stood.

We now bought land in the town of Chascomús and commenced to build a house. Here we had more trouble, for a man whom I will call 'Fox' made a bother as about the measurement of the land, saying that we were taking more than we were entitled to. I need not go into details, but I knew he was wrong and that the piece of land was legally ours. I called someone on my side, and he did on his. The morning we arranged to meet to settle the question was, I think, the coldest I have ever experienced; I was frozen. I had made little flags to mark the boundary. Well, sometimes right triumphs over might, and it was soon agreed that the land was ours. I will relate an incident in connection with this man 'Fox'. He and his family were Roman Catholics. One day 'Fox' was very ill and his life in danger. Some friends asked me if I was going to see him, and I said, 'No.' At last his wife sent for me and I went, for she and I were quite good friends, as we had always been, and the poor woman felt the wrong doing of 'Fox'. When I arrived, I found the wife in great distress. She told me her husband was passing away and that he had received the Host, and begged me to go into the room. I did so, and found him lying seemingly unconscious and faintly moaning. Round the bed, waiting for him to breathe his last, were twelve Irishmen. I went to the bedside and putting my hand on his chest gave him a shake and said, 'Do you know who is speaking to you?'. No notice. I then repeated the shake a little harder. He opened his eyes and on seeing me gave a start of recognition and said, 'You, Mrs. Robson.' I said, 'Yes, it is.' He said, 'I have done you a lot of harm and now I am dying, but do me one favour; I feel starving, give me a piece of tobacco.' This was an odd request from a dying man. However, I turned to ask one of the men for some and one of them leaned forward and gave him a piece; he chewed it ravenously. I thought, 'This is strange, it looks more as if the man is starving', so I called for some soup and gave him a spoonful and he drank it down. There was a horrified exclamation from them all; how wrong to give him this, after he had received the last sacrament. I said, 'Oh, the charm was broken by the tobacco.' I remained an hour, giving him a spoonful of soup at short intervals, which was continued after I left by his wife. There was no wake this time, for 'Fox' recovered and lived for 16 years after this, and alas, to do me more mischief.

Our house was eventually finished in Chascomús, and very comfortable and roomy it is, and it is very nice having my children coming to see me. My daughter Euphemia and her little baby a fortnight old were staying with me; she had left her little family at home to be looked after. They were all well and happy till one evening when they were playing in a room with a fire, for it was cold weather. There was a kettle of boiling water on the fire. Whilst romping, one of the children pulled it down and the whole of its contents fell on a little girl (Nellie) who was near. There was great excitement and alarm, of course, and a boy was sent off for me. My daughter and I were sitting quietly when I heard a lot of talking and hurried out, for I was anxious that my daughter should not be alarmed. The messenger explained what had happened. I tried to keep it from my daughter but she became so agitated, fearing that something had happened to her children, that I told her. We started immediately for the house, and when we arrived it was a sad thing for the mother to find her little girl in such a state of suffering. Her poor little arm was very badly scalded. I dressed it as well as I could till the Doctor arrived and then took her home with us. I dressed it twice a day under the Doctor's orders. The poor little thing did not like to see me coming, for, of course, I had to give her some pain. She would say, 'No, no, Granny, baa baa', which meant in her baby language, 'I want to go to sleep.' It was a mercy her face escaped scalding or she would have been terribly disfigured. As it is one arm is much marked and she can never wear short sleeves.

About 1881 I had gone out to the *estancia* for a few days to super-intend some work I wanted done. Amongst other things there were some trees to be felled, and I told the peon who was doing them that I would go out and see it done. A Mr. G. and his little girl were there, and we were all standing watching the felling of the trees. Mr. G. was nearer the tree than I was. I saw it falling, and at the same moment Mr. G. saw it coming and ran to get clear of it. His little girl seeing him run dashed after him, thus taking her into the danger line. I made a rush to catch her and seizing her flung her away, and thus saved her, but there was not time for me to get away, and down the tree came, crash, on my head. They told me afterwards that it was some little time before the peon and Mr. G. could remove the tree to extricate me, and when they did they thought I was dead, for I looked so white and was quite unconscious. I had a terrible cut on the top of my head, and a handkerchief which I had tied on my head was buried in the wound. When I partially recovered my senses, the blood was rushing down my face. They tried to stop it with cold water, but this made me feel I was going mad, so I let it bleed, and as soon as I could get into the house I applied a cloth dipped in hot water. For some days I felt very ill and could only keep quiet. I had no Doctor, but cured the cut myself with applications of kerosene. I always date my deafness as from this time, for a great noise started in my head and I have never been free from it since, and shortly after I became deaf. This has been a great trial to me. None but those who are deaf can realise what a drawback deafness is. I do like to enter into all that is going on and enjoy the fun and brightness of all my young people. I returned to Chascomús as soon as I was able, and found my husband and Dr. R. playing chess. They were alarmed when they saw my bandaged head. I soon assured them that I was far on the road to recovery, and after showing the Doctor my head I told him how I had cured it myself with a simple remedy.

I am nearly at the end of this record of my life. I have gone through many troubled waters, as I have related, and there are many I have not mentioned. When I settled in my house in Chascomús with every comfort around me, I hoped my life had settled into a calm and peaceful one, but there were still a few more battles to be fought and won.

For many years we had our services and Sunday School in a room at the Manse, but there arose reasons why this was not convenient and must be discontinued, so I determined to build a hall of my own. We commenced to raise money and I got up a subscription dance which proved most successful and was enjoyed by a large company. I was rather troubled and could not help thinking of a very disagreeable meeting which I had to attend the next day. I wished to erect a vault in our Scottish burial ground, and this had been strongly opposed by a great many of the members of the Church. I had been working hard for it. Well, this final meeting was held to settle it all. When it came to the holding up of hands, for and against, I was hurt to see many who had enjoyed the dance only the evening before, appearing against me. Amongst others there, were my good and life-long friends, Mr. and Mrs. B. Partially, I think, through Mr. B.'s help, the vote was given in my favour after all. I have built my vault, and many members of my family are resting in it, and when my end comes I hope to be taken there.

For some years now my life has run an even course – as smoothly as it could with a large family (amongst whom I have 60 great-grandchildren) and in whom I am always greatly interested and whose joys and sorrows are mine.

It is now 1908. On St. Andrew's day in the afternoon we had tea and games and prizes for the children at the Manse. In the evening we had a large dance at the Robson Hall, which was greatly enjoyed by us all. In the summer of this year we had a service in our Church, with the Holy Communion, followed by a ceremony of unveiling two memorial tablets – one to the memory of 'Padre' Smith and the other to Mr. Ferguson, the minister who preceded our present one. Two of the oldest members of the Scottish community unveiled them, Mr. Brown was one and I the other.

I must mention before closing that there are many nights when I cannot sleep. I get up and write what I call my thoughts, but my friends call poetry. A friend was struck with, and much interested in, some lines I wrote on the death of our beloved Queen Victoria and asked to be allowed to send them home to King Edward VII, which she did. To my surprise and gratification I received a letter quite soon dated from Buckingham Palace acknowledging and accepting the lines. Needless to say it is a treasured possession.

On my 89th birthday I gave a dance at which my old friends and neighbours, Mr. and Mrs. Brown, and my dear old friend Mrs. Buchanan, were present, and among the many guests were included my son and daughters, grandchildren and great-grandchildren, and I look forward to our meeting again to see the young folk dance and enjoy themselves.

THE END

Tam o' Stirling's Poetic Account of the Voyage of the *Symmetry*[1]
(transcribed from James Dodds, *Records of the Scottish Settlers*, pp. 24–
26)

> Frae the land o' brown heath and tartan plaids,
> Frae the Country o' cakes and barley bannocks,
> A comely selection o' chields[2] and maids,
> On board of the *Symmetry* swung their ham'ocks.
>
> The emigrants all were a worthy crew,
> Frae south and west whom none surpasses,
> Where braxy mutton[3] and mountain dew
> Rear sturdy callants[4] and strappin' lasses.
>
> Farmers and blacksmiths, prize ploughmen were there,
> Dairymaids fresh as the butter they made,

1. It is tempting to speculate as to the identity of 'Tam o' Stirling' on the basis of Dodds's passenger list. Starting from the assumptions that his forename was Thomas, that he was a native of the Stirling area, and that he possessed sufficient learning to be versed in the art of poetry, he may have been Thomas Galbraith, one of the eight principal members of the colony. The Galbraiths were a prominent Stirling dynasty at that time, the male members of which would have received a solid grounding in grammatical and literary studies at the town's respected school, where Latin and Greek were the main subjects. Although I have found no conclusive proof that the Thomas Galbraith who ventured to Argentina hailed from this family, there is some circumstantial evidence to support my hypothesis, such as the facts that as one of the leaders of the Monte Grande party he would almost certainly have come from an affluent background, and that the name Thomas does appear in records of the Stirling Galbraiths, albeit more commonly as a middle name.
2. *chield*: in this context, a young man.
3. *braxy mutton*: meat, usually salted, from a sheep which has died a natural death, hence old and tough.
4. *callant*: lad.

Guidwives[5] wi' their weans,[6] sae rosy and fair,
And the honest guidman[7] wi' his collie and spade.

As Scotia's shores were receding behind them,
And the *Symmetry* furrowed along through the foam,
Each felt that no poet required to remind them,
That ever so humble there is no place like home.

And the elders confessed, as each blew his nose,
And stealthily wiping a trickling tear,
That darling Auld Scotland wi' skim milk an' brose,[8]
Wad beat Buenos Aires and five hunder[9] a year.

But sailing along we got soon reconciled,
As daily some wonder enchanted our view,
While frolicsome chappies the evenings beguiled
Wi' gruesome ghost stories they guaranteed true.

At length Biscay Bay, that dread o' the sailor,
They entered, and lo! old Neptune was frowning,
Huge waves turned the cheeks of pluckiest paler,
And every one thought 'twas a matter of drowning.

Three days of tossing, sea-sick and forlorn,
A storm on the sea and a deil[10] in their stomachs,
The emigrants wished they had never been born
Tae be buffeted thus, and chucked frae their hammocks.

Wrathful surges becalmed, bright Phoebus[11] appearing,
And storm-tossed emigrants crawled up on deck,

5. *guidwife*: woman farmer or farmer's wife.
6. *wean*: child.
7. *guidman*: small farmer.
8. *brose*: oatmeal or peasemeal mixed with boiling water or milk to make a type of porridge.
9. *hunder*: hundred.
10. *deil*: devil.
11. *Phoebus*: an epithet of Apollo, employed when the god is identified with the sun. The presence of this classical allusion may lend further weight to my conjecture regarding the educational background of 'Tam o' Stirling' (see note 1).

They sang the ship's praises, and lustily cheering
Brave Cochrane the Captain wi' deepest respec'.[12]

They assisted the crew wi' a 'Yoh heave ho,'
They played pitch and toss and primitive skittles,
But soon *Symmeterians* got wisely to know
That at sea the finest diversion is victuals.

For sickness o'er and their appetites whetted,
Puir[13] cookie was hunted frae aft to the fore,
Eating was trumps, and the steward he fretted
That famine would board them ere reaching the shore.

But useless his fears, for a special tuck in
O' crackers and junk[14] soon settled the matter,
'Twas saltish nae doubt, but cook said, wi' a grin,
That the *Symmetry* carried abundance o' water.

For ploughmen accustomed to parritch[15] and kail[16]
Found petrified biscuits dourish[17] tae munch,
While ancient salt pork made their appetites fail
And willingly tackle the pump for their lunch.

They wondered what people the Argentines were,
Savage or civilised – colour, and figure,

12. It is curious to note that the Captain is identified as Cochrane here, given that Grierson calls him Smith. In *Records of the Scottish Settlers*, Dodds also asserts that the *Symmetry* was under the command of 'William (familiarly called "Wullie") Cochrane . . . – an honest Scot and jolly tar as ever paced a quarterdeck, symmetrical in all his bearings as his own good ship' (p. 11). An explanation of this discrepancy can be found in Cecilia Grierson's *Colonia de Monte Grande: Primera y única colonia formada por escoceses en la Argentina* (Buenos Aires: Peuser, 1925), where she asserts that Cochrane was the *Symmetry*'s regular captain, but that he was replaced by Smith for the voyage to Buenos Aires on account of his advanced age (p. 41).
13. *Puir*: poor.
14. *junk*: a nautical term denoting hard, salted meat.
15. *parritch*: porridge.
16. *kail*: kale; broth made of kale and other greens.
17. *dourish*: quite hard.

And lassies resolved they would droon[18] themselves ere
They'd gang[19] without claes[20] or be kissed by a nigger.

One morning the emigrants arose wi' delight,
And joy did prevail 'mongst the *Symmetry*'s crew,
As the topman hailed deck, Montevideo in sight,
Though nought could be seen but a thin streak o' blue.

Then all was activity, bustle, commotion
Of premature packing and donning o' braws,[21]
Seemingly having adopted the notion
O' flying ashore wi' the gulls and sea-maws.[22]

For leagues lay between them and Argentine's shore,
And days would still pass ere they anchored off there,
But each morning the colonists packed as before,
And nightly unbundled again in despair.

Till bowling along up the billowy Plate,
The *Symmetry* struck wi' a shudder and clank,
While the pilot he swore 'twas the trick'ry o' fate
Lured the Britishers on to the 'English Bank.'

Great was the wailing, on this sudden disaster,
Tae stick in midstream as they neared Buenos Aires,
And all save wee Tammy, the daft poetaster,
Took to reading their bibles and saying their prayers.

At length they got off and free from the danger,
Hearts filled wi' delight as they sighted the shore,
Their land of adoption, home of the stranger,
From where they would ne'er go to sea any more.

18. *droon*: drown.
19. *gang*: go.
20. *claes*: clothes.
21. *braws*: fine clothes.
22. *maw*: the common gull.

The *Symmetry* anchored, boats gathered around them,
While jabbering foreigners their luggage received,
The Babel o' tongues was enough to confound them,
But naebody understood Scotch, they perceived.

Betimes there started a coo-cairt[23] procession,
O' colonists, implements, bedding, and rations,
Bound for the South, where the Robertson concession
Awaited to welcome the Scotch Immigration.

23. *coo-cairt*: cart drawn by a cow or bullock.

APPENDIX 2

Selected Details of the Background and Life of William Grierson (transcribed from Cecilia Grierson, *Colonia de Monte Grande*, and translated from the original Spanish)

The Robertsons appointed their friend and, I believe, relative William Grierson to purchase in Edinburgh and Dumfries the most indispensable agricultural implements and domestic equipment for those [prospective members of the Monte Grande colony] who could not afford them personally, and entrusted him with the task of organisation, at least until the colonists arrived at their destination.

A short time after their arrival, my father was born and was baptised in the British Consulate. The name and surname of his godfather were placed before that of his father . . . He was called, therefore, John Parish Robertson Grierson. Educated in England, he dedicated his adult life to *estancia* work and to breeding race horses. He and his brothers were considered the best 'gentlemen riders' of the era, according to accounts published recently. After the battle of Caseros, he succeeded in winning for Buenos Aires the challenge race against the men who had accompanied General Urquiza, the most talked-about contest of the time.[1] (pp. 38–39)

My grandparents [were] direct descendants of Sir Robert Grierson, Laird of Lag (Grier of Lag in the novels of Walter Scott), their ancestry stained by neither blot nor blemish since 1314. They were related to the first Duke of Queensbury [*sic*] and had served their King and been martyrs for their religion in the time of the 'covenanters', as official documents

1. Justo José de Urquiza, the Federalist governor of Entre Ríos Province, became aggrieved by the favouritism Rosas displayed towards Buenos Aires. In response, Urquiza rebelled and finally vanquished the dictator in 1852 at Caseros, not far from Buenos Aires, thus ending the latter's despotic reign. Following the defeat, Rosas fled to England, where he spent the remainder of his days in exile.

and tombstones in Dumfries cemetery reveal, on which the following names appear frequently: Grierson, Jardine, Montgomerie, Hamilton, Hope Johnstone, the Earls of Annandale, etc. (p. 58)

APPENDIX 3

William Grierson's Obituary from *The British Packet*, 31 January 1847 (transcribed from James Dodds, *Records of the Scottish Settlers*, pp. 229-30)

Died, at Monte Grande, on 29th January 1847, in consequence of a fall from his horse, Mr. William Grierson, a native of Dumfriesshire, Scotland. His loss will be severely felt in the neighbourhood and community with which he was connected.

Active and intelligent in all rural affairs, his advice was freely tendered and his assistance freely lent. To the independence of character distinctive of the British yeoman Mr. Grierson added that equanimity of temper, blandness of manners, and cheerfulness of disposition which impart a charm to social intercourse. Frank, generous, and hospitable, he enjoyed the respect and friendship of a wide circle of acquaintances. The estimation in which he was held by his fellow-countrymen may safely be inferred from the general interest excited by his melancholy accident, the sympathy evinced for his sorrowing family, and the very large and respectable attendance that accompanied his mortal remains to their last resting-place.

These spontaneous demonstrations of respect are reserved exclusively for personal worth; rank cannot command and wealth cannot purchase them. During life the awards of public opinion may be warped by accidental influences, but when the different classes of a community concur in testifying to the worth and respectability of the departed, it is clear and conclusive proof that he possessed some positive and well-established claims to their good opinions. The selfish and overbearing may live by himself and for himself, but his death must be in keeping with his life. So true is it, even in the world, that 'whatsoever a man soweth, the same shall he reap.'

BIBLIOGRAPHY OF WORKS
CITED OR CONSULTED

Anderson, Benedict, *Imagined Communities: Reflections on the Origin and Spread of Nationalism*, revised edn (London: Verso, 1991)

Assunçao, Fernando *El gaucho*, 2 vols (Montevideo: Dirección General de Extensión Universitaria, 1978)

Bailey, John P., 'Inmigración y relaciones étnicas. Los ingleses en la Argentina', *Desarrollo Económico* (Buenos Aires) 18 (1979), 539-58

Beaumont, J. A. B., *Travels in Buenos Ayres and the Adjacent Provinces of the Río de la Plata with Observations intended for the use of Persons who Contemplate Emigrating to that Country or Embarking Capital in its Affairs* (London: James Ridgway, 1828)

Bethell, Leslie (ed.), *Argentina Since Independence* (Cambridge: Cambridge University Press, 1993)

Bustamante, José Luis, *Los cinco errores capitales de la intervención anglo-francesa en el Plata* (Buenos Aires: Solar, 1942)

Craig, Alexander, 'Scotland and Argentina', *Scottish Field*, October 1966, pp. 38-39

Darwin, Charles, *The Voyage of the Beagle* (London: Heron Books, 1968)

Dodds, James, *Records of the Scottish Settlers on the River Plate and their Churches* (Buenos Aires: Grant and Sylvester, 1897)

Ferns, H. S., 'Britain's Informal Empire in Argentina, 1806-1914', *Past and Present*, 4 (1954), 60-75

———— *Britain and Argentina in the Nineteenth Century* (Oxford: Clarendon Press, 1960)

Fletcher, Ian, *The Waters of Oblivion: The British Invasion of the Río de la Plata, 1806-1807* (Tunbridge Wells: Spellmount, 1991)

Fox, Everett (ed.), *The Five Books of Moses: Genesis, Exodus, Leviticus, Numbers, and Deuteronomy* (London: The Harvill Press, 1995)

Gálvez, Manuel, *Vida de don Juan Manuel de Rosas* (Buenos Aires: Fontis, 1975)

Gibson, Herbert, *The History and Present State of the Sheep-Breeding Industry in the Argentine Republic* (Buenos Aires: Ravenscroft and Mills, 1893)

Graham-Yooll, Andrew, '¡Llegaron los escoceses!: A 150 años del arribo del "Symmetry"', *Clarín* (Buenos Aires), 21 August 1975, p. 8

_____ *The Forgotten Colony: A History of the English-Speaking Communities in Argentina* (London: Hutchinson, 1981)

Grant, William Denis, 'A History of St. Andrew's Presbyterian Church in Argentina, Chapter 1', in the November–December 1989 issue of the newsletter of the Iglesia Presbiteriana San Andrés, Buenos Aires, pp. 8–11

Grierson, Cecilia, *Colonia de Monte Grande: Primera y única colonia formada por escoceses en la Argentina* (Buenos Aires: Peuser, 1925)

Halperín-Donghi, Tulio, *Politics, Economics and Society in Argentina in the Revolutionary Period* (Cambridge: Cambridge University Press, 1975)

Hudson, W. H., *Far Away and Long Ago: A Childhood in Argentina* (London: Century Hutchinson, 1985)

Ibarguren, Carlos, *Juan Manuel de Rosas: su vida, su tiempo, su drama*, 2nd edn (Buenos Aires: Roldán, 1930)

Jones, Wilbur Devereux, 'The Argentine British Colony in the Time of Rosas', *Hispanic American Historical Review*, 40 (1960), 90–97

Lynch, John, *Argentine Dictator: Juan Manuel de Rosas 1829-1852* (Oxford: Clarendon Press, 1981)

Macinnes, Allan I., and others (eds.), *Scottish Migration to the Americas, c. 1650-1939: A Documentary Source Book* (Edinburgh: Pillans and Wilson, forthcoming)

Mackenzie, Greta, *Why Patagonia?* (Stornoway: *Stornoway Gazette*, 1995)

Mair, Craig, *David Angus: The Life and Adventures of a Victorian Railway Engineer* (Stevenage: The Strong Oak Press, 1989)

Masefield, John, *The Collected Poems of John Masefield* (London: William Heinemann, 1932)

Miller, Rory, *Britain and Latin America in the Nineteenth and Twentieth Centuries* (London: Longman, 1993)

Muñoz Azpiri, José Luis, *Rosas frente al imperio británico* (Buenos Aires: Theoría, 1974)

Oddone, Juan Antonio, *La emigración europea al Río de la Plata: Motivaciones y proceso de incorporación* (Montevideo: Ediciones de la Banda Oriental, 1966)

Reader's Digest Guide to Places of the World: A Geographical Dictionary of Countries, Cities, Natural and Man-made Wonders (London: Reader's Digest Association, 1987)

Sarmiento, Domingo Faustino, *Facundo* (Madrid: Cátedra, 1993)

Shumway, Nicolas, *The Invention of Argentina* (Berkeley, Los Angeles, London: University of California Press, 1991)

Slatta, Richard W., *Gauchos and the Vanishing Frontier* (Lincoln, Nebraska, and London: University of Nebraska Press, 1983)

Stewart, Iain A. D., 'Living with Dictator Rosas: Argentina through Scottish Eyes', *Journal of Latin American Studies* 29 (1997), 23-44

———— 'Textual Representations of Religion in Rosas' Argentina', *Bulletin of Hispanic Studies* 74 (1997), 483-500

Szuchman, Mark D. and Jonathon C. Brown (eds.), *Revolution and Restoration: The Rearrangement of Power in Argentina, 1776-1860* (Lincoln, Nebraska, and London: University of Nebraska Press, 1994)

The Concise Scots Dictionary (Aberdeen: Aberdeen University Press, 1985)

The Oxford English Reference Dictionary (Oxford: Oxford University Press, 1995)

Walker, John (ed.), *The Scottish Sketches of R. B. Cunninghame Graham* (Edinburgh: Scottish Academic Press, 1982)

Wolf, Ema and Cristina Patriarca, *La gran inmigración* (Buenos Aires: Sudamericana, 1991)

INDEX